a beautiful pea green boat

wrapped up in a £5 note

and say to a small guitar

a lovely pussy you are

glove with a ring through the end of
his nose.

ART AT AUCTION 1985–86

Honoré Daumier
LE DÉFENSEUR À LA BARRE
Pen and black, reddish-brown and blue ink, and ink wash on laid paper, signed, 7⅝in by 9½in
(19.4cm by 24.2cm)
New York $253,000 (£165,359). 14.V.86
From the collection of the late Jean S. Alexander

Opposite
Henri de Toulouse-Lautrec
AU BAL DE L'OPÉRA
Peinture à l'essence and charcoal heightened with white gouache on buff paper laid on board,
signed, signed with monogram and dated '*93*, 31⅛in by 19⅞in (79cm by 50.5cm)
New York $2,860,000 (£1,857,143). 13.V.86
From the collection of the late Willavene S. Morris

Well known society figures are portrayed in this picture, including Jane Avril the celebrated
dancer at the Moulin Rouge, who appears in the foreground with her back to the spectator.
Standing beside her in the centre is Maurice Guibert, a representative of Moët and Chandon and
friend of the artist, and in the background, seated by the balustrade, is the Prince de Sagan.

Camille Pissarro
AVENUE DE L'OPÉRA, PLACE DU THÉÂTRE FRANÇAIS, TEMPS BRUMEUX
Signed and dated '*98*, 29in by 36in (73.7cm by 91.5cm)
New York $1,540,000 (£1,000,000). 13.V.86
From the collection of Mr and Mrs David Bakalar

Pissarro began painting Parisian scenes relatively late in his career, in 1893, thirty years after
Manet, Monet and Renoir had painted the same theme. On 15 December 1897, he wrote, '. . . I
found a room in the Grand Hôtel du Louvre with a superb view of the Avenue de l'Opéra and the
corner of the Place du Palais Royal. It is very beautiful to paint. Perhaps it is not aesthetic, but I
am delighted to be able to paint these Paris streets that people have come to call ugly, but which
are so silvery, so luminous and vital.' (*Lettres*, pp. 441–2).

Paul Signac
BRISE
Signed, dated '*91* and inscribed *Op. 222*, 25⅝in by 32¼in (65cm by 82cm)
London £726,000 ($1,132,560). 3.XII.85
From the collection of the late Sir Charles Clore

Signac sent a sequence of five pictures to the *Exposition des XX* in Brussels in 1892 entitled *La Mer, Les Barques*, painted in Concarneau, Brittany, in 1891. To each he gave musical terms as titles, 'Scherzo', 'Larghetto', 'Allegro maestoso', 'Adagio' and 'Presto'. He was at that time studying the analogies of rhythm and harmony in painting and music. A few months later, at the *Exposition des Indépendants*, he changed the titles to more descriptive ones, this picture becoming *Brise*.

Pierre-Auguste Renoir
BAIGNEUSE (FEMME EN JUPE ROUGE S'ESSUYANT LES PIEDS)
Signed, *circa* 1888, 26in by 20in (66cm by 50.8cm)
New York $1,650,000 (£1,161,972). 13.XI.85
From the collection of Elliot and Ruth Handler

Opposite
Claude Monet
TROIS PEUPLIERS, EFFET D'AUTOMNE
Signed and dated '*91*, 36¼in by 28¾in (92cm by 73cm)
New York $1,540,000 (£1,084,507). 13.XI.85
From the collection of Albert J. Dreitzer

Henri Fantin-Latour
FLEURS ET FRUITS
Signed and dated '68, 21¾in by 21½in (55.2cm by 54.7cm)
New York $1,540,000 (£1,000,000). 13.V.86
From the collection of Mr and Mrs David Bakalar

Pierre Bonnard
LA NAPPE À CARREAUX
Signed, 1916, 18¼in by 21¾in (46.4cm by 55.3cm)
New York $462,000 (£300,000). 13.V.86
From the collection of the late Etta E. Steinberg

Henri Martin
GABRIELLE AT THE GARDEN DOOR
Signed and dated *1910*, 79⅛in by 41½in
(201cm by 105.4cm)
London £165,000 ($260,700). 25.VI.86

Mikhail Larionov
COSTUME DESIGN FOR 'LA FEMME DU VIEUX BOUFFON' IN THE BALLET 'CHOUT'
Watercolour and charcoal, signed, and inscribed on the backboard, *circa* 1921,
14½in by 9⅝in (36.9cm by 24.5cm)
New York $30,800 (£20,131). 23.IV.86

Robert Delaunay
STUDY FOR 'LES FENÊTRES'
Watercolour, signed and dated *juin 1912*
14½in by 32⅞in (37cm by 83.5cm)
London £132,000 ($204,600). 5.XII.85

This watercolour is one of three which are all closely related to the painting *Fenêtres en Trois Parties*, in the Philadelphia Museum of Art.

Opposite
Juan Gris
VIOLON ET GRAVURE ACCROCHÉE
Oil, sand and collage on canvas, signed and dated *4–13* on the reverse, 25⅝in by 19⅝in
(65cm by 50cm)
London £1,375,000 ($2,172,500). 24.VI.86

Some months after this picture was completed, Gris wrote in a letter to Kahnweiler that he felt that a fragment of a different image could be attached instead of the engraving in the frame in the background without damage to the overall character of the picture '. . . once Mr Brenner is the owner of the picture, he is at liberty to substitute something else for this engraving – even his own portrait if he likes. It may look better, or it may look worse . . . but it won't upset the actual merits of the picture.' Happily, no substitution for the engraving has ever been made.

Gino Severini
LE WAGON DE PREMIÈRE CLASSE DU NORD-SUD
On panel, signed, and signed and titled on the reverse, 1912, 14⅜in by 22⅜in (36.5cm by 57cm)
London £192,500 ($304,150). 24.VI.86

Painted in 1912 in Paris, this is one of a group of futurist works based on the motives of *velocità e rumore* on the themes of the *Autobus* and the *Nord-Sud* metro line.

Opposite
Johannes Baader
DADA MILCHSTRASSE
Collage, signed and inscribed *Diese Dinge haben Dadaland vorbereitet am 7, 320, circa* 1920,
19¾in by 12¼in (50cm by 32.5cm)
London £55,000 ($85,250). 4.XII.85

Ernst Ludwig Kirchner
EINRADFAHRER
Stamped with the estate stamp on the reverse, 1911, 33¾in by 37½in (85.7cm by 95.2cm)
New York $649,000 (£457,042). 13.XI.85
From the collection of Mr Gordon F. Hampton

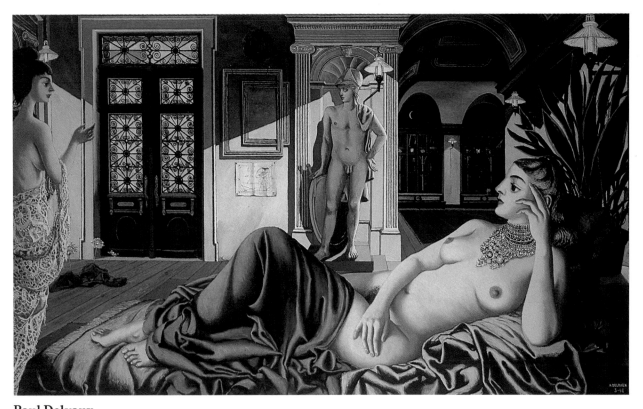

Paul Delvaux
L'ÉLOGE DE LA MÉLANCOLIE
On panel, signed, titled and dated *3–48*, 60⅛in by 100⅜in (153cm by 255cm)
London £302,500 ($471,900). 3.XII.85

Ernst Barlach
RUSSISCHES BAUERNPAAR
Pencil, signed, 1907, 17½in by 25in (44.5cm by 63.3cm)
London £28,600 ($43,758). 26.III.86
From the collection of Mark Roland

Opposite
Egon Schiele
PORTRAIT OF JOHANN HARMS
Watercolour, gouache and pencil on paper, signed and dated *1916*, 19in by 12⅜in
(48.3cm by 31.4cm)
New York $693,000 (£488,028). 14.XI.85
From the collection of George Moore

This is probably the final study for Schiele's portrait of his father-in-law Johann Harms.

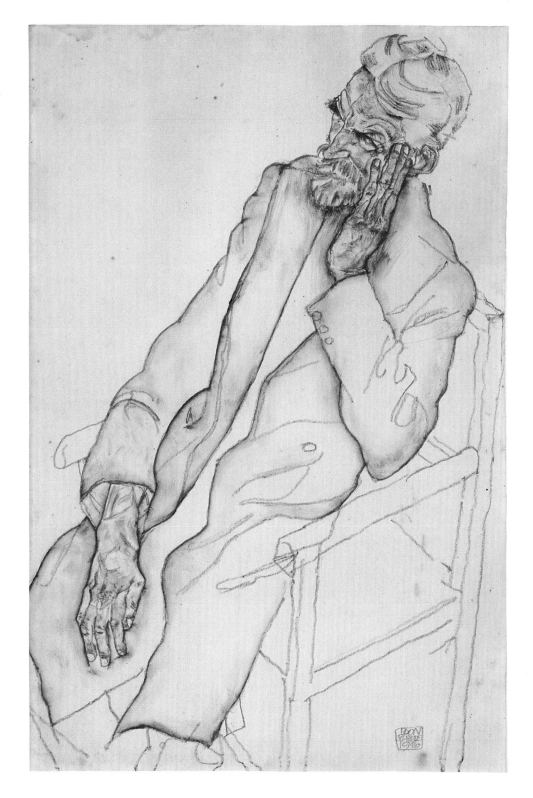

Henry Moore
TWO PIECE RECLINING FIGURE NO.2
Bronze, signed, numbered *7/7* and inscribed with the foundry mark *Noack Berlin*, 1960,
length 102in (259cm)
New York $935,000 (£607,143). 13.V.86

Ben Nicholson
ROOFTOPS ST. IVES
Signed, dated *May 19–48 St. Ives* on the canvas overlap, signed and inscribed *Chy an Kerrie Carbis*
Bay Cornwall on the stretcher, and signed, titled and dated on the backboard, $17\frac{7}{8}$in by $27\frac{1}{2}$in
(45.5cm by 70cm)
London £118,800 ($185,328). 3.XII.85
From the collection of the late Sir Charles Clore

Cy Twombly
UNTITLED
Oil, pencil and red pencil on canvas, signed and dated *1956*, 50in by 62¾in (127cm by 159.4cm)
New York $418,000 (£292,308). 5.XI.85
From the collection of the Dia Art Foundation

Arshile Gorky
UNTITLED
Oil on cardboard, signed and dated '*44*, 23½in by 29¾in (59.7cm by 75.6cm)
New York $440,000 (£307,692). 5.XI.85

Jasper Johns
PAINTING WITH RULER AND 'GRAY'
Oil and collage with objects on canvas, signed, titled and dated *1960* on the reverse, 32in by 32in
(81.2cm by 81.2cm)
New York $687,500 (£480,769). 5.XI.85

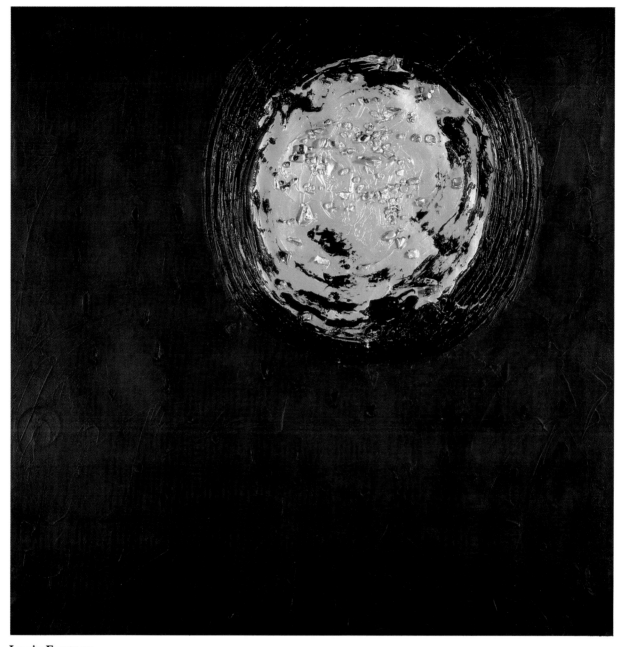

Lucio Fontana
LUNA A VENEZIA
Oil and glass pebbles on canvas, signed and titled on the reverse, 1961, 59in by 59in (150cm by 150cm)
London £143,000 ($225,940). 26.VI.86

Howard Hodgkin
PORTRAIT OF MR AND MRS KASMIN
Signed on the reverse, titled and dated *1964–6* on the stretcher, 41¾in by 50in (106cm by 127cm)
London £66,000 ($102,300). 5.XII.85

Opposite
Hans Hofmann
SWAMP-ELEGY
Signed and dated *'62*, and signed, titled, dated *1962* and numbered *1436* on the reverse,
50in by 40in (127cm by 101.6cm)
New York $242,000 (£157,143). 5.V.86
From the collection of the late Willavene S. Morris

Serge Poliakoff
COMPOSITION
Signed, 1969, 64⅛in by 51¼in (163cm by 130cm)
London £83,600 ($132,088). 26.VI.86

Asger Jorn
LE MOMENT CHOISIT
Signed, and signed, titled and dated '71 on the reverse, 83¾in by 67in (213.3cm by 170.2cm)
London £104,500 ($161,975). 5.XII.85

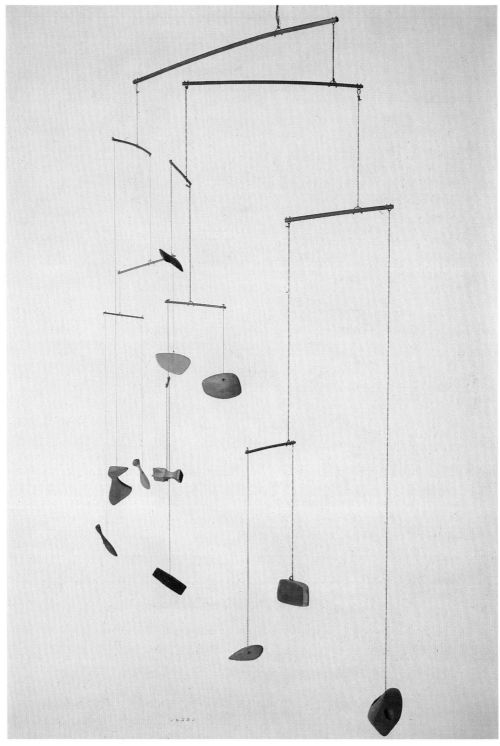

Alexander Calder
UNTITLED
Painted wood mobile, *circa* 1940, 84in by 59in (213.3cm by 149.9cm)
New York $198,000 (£128,571). 5.V.86
From the collection of Henrique E. Mindlin

Jean Tinguely
FONTAINE F
Iron wheels, metal rods, rubber belts and tube with electric motor, 1968,
height 106¼in (270cm)
London £59,400 ($93,852). 26.VI.86

Rubens Peale with a geranium by Rembrandt Peale

Carol Eaton Hevner

In the preface to his *Portfolio of an Artist* (1839) Rembrandt Peale declared that, 'The beautiful creations of this world are chiefly manifested through the sense of sight, and especially all that relates to form and colour, distance and light, and shade; . . .' To capture the beauty that the eye perceives in nature was clearly Peale's aim in this intimate and carefully painted portrait of his seventeen-year-old brother, Rubens (Fig. 1). The sense of sight is gratified by subtle contrasts of colour, texture and form; the depiction of the soft textures of flesh, geranium leaves, velvet collar and tousled locks of hair are played off against the less yielding metal spectacles, ceramic pot and hard twisting stems. Here beauty has been found not in an exalted theme but in the simple facts of a familiar world.

Twenty-three-year-old Rembrandt Peale was well aware of European academic prescriptions for high art and his career soon showed that his aims lay in that direction. Yet, this is a different sort of painting. Its strength comes from the artist's immediate and uninhibited approach to the subject and in his use of light and colour. An ability to record with the directness and veracity seen here was an artistic value often praised by Rembrandt's father, Charles Willson Peale (1741–1827), and in this painting Rembrandt expresses much of the Peale family's attitudes, interests and tender regard for one another.

Born in Maryland, Charles Willson Peale studied the theory and practice of painting in Benjamin West's London studio and conveyed to his family both a love of art as well as a belief in its social utility. Married three times, the elder Peale fathered eleven children who survived past infancy. Nearly all of them painted to some extent, as did many of his grandchildren. Charles Willson Peale's work divides into essentially three categories: elegant yet genial depictions of the Maryland and Philadelphia gentry, portraits of men of political, scientific or cultural importance and intimate yet realistic portraits of the immediate family. It is to this last group that Rembrandt's portrait of his brother is indebted.

C.W. Peale's hopes for his talented son Rembrandt's artistic career were almost unbounded. This may have been due, in part, to his disappointment over the career of his eldest son Raphaelle (1774–1825) whose self-indulgence and predilection for still-life painting did not equate with Charles' ideas of a healthy, productive and socially useful life. Ironically, the works Raphaelle left behind reveal him to be America's consummate still-life painter. Sensuous, witty and beautifully constructed, his compositions transcend the sum of the simple objects they contain.

Fig. 1
Rembrandt Peale
RUBENS PEALE WITH A GERANIUM
Signed *Rem. Peale* and dated *1801*, 28in by 24in (71.1cm by 61cm)
New York $4,070,000 (£2,750,000). 5.XII.85

This painting is now in the National Gallery of Art, Washington DC.

As his talented sons grew to maturity, Peale painted less and his interests changed. In 1786 he opened the Philadelphia Museum with the aim of enlightening the public. Here he hung portraits he had painted of the leaders of the American Revolution. To them he added scientific specimens he had collected, reflecting his growing interest in the natural sciences, a preoccupation which led to friendships with some of the most eminent international scientists of his day. Peale's 1822 self-portrait (Fig. 2) portrays his dual interests in natural science and art. Rubens shared his father's fascination for the natural sciences and between 1810 and the financial collapse of 1839, he successively ran Peale Museums in Philadelphia, Baltimore and New York. Only in later life did he begin to paint, instructed by his daughter Mary Jane.

From his youth, Rubens delighted in plants. Philadelphia was then the horticultural capital of the United States due to the activities of the Bartrams, father and son, who dedicated their lives to searching out native plants and importing species from abroad. Geraniums, native and imported were extant in America before 1801. Mary Jane Peale in her listing of the paintings she owned in 1883, declared the variety Rubens proudly displays to be the first Scarlet Geranium in America, which he had succeeded in raising from seed. This may have provided the inspiration for Rembrandt's portrait. Rubens' eyesight had always been poor and he was originally painted holding his spectacles but it was later decided that he would look more like himself with them on. When the second pair was added, the first were never deleted.

Rembrandt Peale's technical knowledge and awareness of the work of the great European masters increased after his trip to England in 1802–1803, and his sojourn in Paris, a few years later, stamped his works with many of the features of Neo-Classicism. His sizeable oeuvre extending from the years 1791 to 1860 contained mainly portraits, but he also produced history painting, landscapes, fancy pieces, copies and variations on the works of the European masters, as well as a small number of still-lifes and miniatures. Together with the most ambitious and talented American painters of his generation such as Washington Allston, Samuel F.B. Morse, Thomas Sully and John Vanderlyn, Peale was keenly aware that American artists must compete with European artists on their terms. As cultural nationalists, these men were intent upon supplying America with a distinguished artistic heritage. Rembrandt painted *Rubens with a geranium* before he became particularly self-conscious about his cultural obligations. His mentors in 1801 were his father and the most famous and sought-after portraitist of the new republic, Gilbert Stuart, who influenced Rembrandt's style between 1795 and 1808.

Rubens with a geranium transcends any singular designation for it unites portraiture with a skilful and evocative still-life. In later years, Rembrandt undoubtedly viewed the painting as one of his less ambitious or culturally important works. In retrospect, however, the spontaneity and feeling he found in this familiar subject have come to be valued as an expression of American artistic sensibility at its best.

Fig. 2
Charles Willson Peale
THE ARTIST IN HIS MUSEUM
1822, 103½in by 80in (263cm by 203.3cm)

Behind the red curtain can be seen Peale's portraits and below them his carefully mounted specimens. To his right is the skeleton of the mastodon he unearthed in upstate New York, and to his left a recently acquired wild turkey and taxidermists' tools.

Reproduced courtesy of the Pennsylvania Academy of the Fine Arts, Joseph and Sarah Harrison Collection.

Thomas Cole
CATSKILL MOUNTAIN HOUSE
1843–44, 28½in by 36½in (72.4cm by 92.7cm)
New York $363,000 (£245,270). 5.XII.85

Albert Bierstadt
VIEW ON THE HUDSON LOOKING ACROSS THE TAPPAN ZEE TOWARDS HOOK MOUNTAIN
Signed and dated *1866*, 36¼in by 72¼in (92cm by 183.7cm)
New York $742,500 (£501,689). 5.XII.85

John George Brown
THE LOST CHILD IN CENTRAL PARK
Signed and dated *1881*, 29in by 44in (73.7cm by 111.7cm)
New York $192,500 (£130,068). 29.V.86

Opposite
John Singer Sargent
MRS CECIL WADE
Signed and dated *1886*, 64in by 53in (162.5cm by 134.6cm)
New York $1,485,000 (£1,003,378). 29.V.86
From the collection of Sir Ruthven Wade

Maurice Brazil Prendergast
LATE AFTERNOON, NEW ENGLAND
Signed, *circa* 1913, 20in by 28in (50.8cm by 71.2cm)
New York $484,000 (£327,027). 5.XII.85

Opposite
Frederick Childe Hassam
FLOWER GIRL
Signed twice and inscribed, 18in by 11in (45.7cm by 27.9cm)
New York $407,000 (£275,000). 5.XII.85

William Merritt Chase
A GRAY DAY IN THE PARK
Signed, and signed, titled and inscribed *51 W. 10th St.* on a label on the reverse, *circa* 1891,
17½in by 17¾in (44.5cm by 45.1cm)
New York $286,000 (£193,243). 29.V.86

Winslow Homer
ENCHANTED
Signed and dated *1874*, 12in by 20in (30.5cm by 50.8cm)
New York $715,000 (£483,108). 5.XII.85

Frederick Frieseke
MISTY MORN
Signed, *circa* 1908, 26in by 32¼in (66cm by 81.9cm)
New York $242,000 (£163,514). 29.V.86

John H. Twachtman
FROM THE UPPER TERRACE
Signed, *circa* 1895, 25in by 30in (63.5cm by 76.2cm)
New York $181,500 (£122,635). 29.V.86
From the collection of the Art Institute of Chicago

Georgia O'Keeffe
WHITE ROSE, NEW MEXICO
Signed on the reverse, titled, inscribed and dated *1930* on a label on the reverse, 30in by 36in
(76.2cm by 91.4cm)
New York $1,265,000 (£854,730). 5.XII.85

Andrew Wyeth
EQUINOX
Tempera on board, signed, 1977, 34½in by 32in (87.6cm by 81.3cm)
New York $264,000 (£178,378). 29.V.86

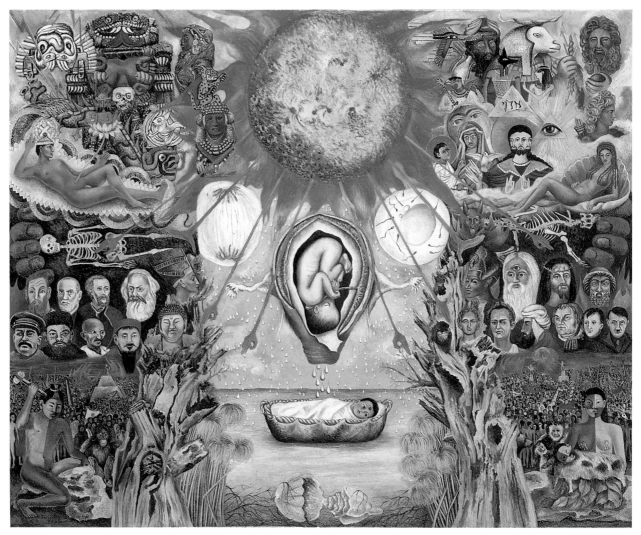

Frida Kahlo
MOSES
Oil on masonite, signed and dated *1945*, 24in by 29¾in (61cm by 75.6cm)
New York $231,000 (£158,219). 26.XI.85

Diego Rivera
LANDSCAPE OF TOLEDO
Signed and dated *1913*, 20$\frac{1}{4}$in by 24$\frac{1}{8}$in (51.5cm by 61.2cm)
New York $220,000 (£150,685). 26.XI.85

Roberto Matta
THE EVE OF DEATH
1938, 28½in by 36⅛in (72.4cm by 91.7cm)
New York $110,000 (£72,848). 20.V.86
From the collection of Gordon Onslow Ford

Rufino Tamayo
MUJERES CANTANDO
Signed and dated *0–40*, 51⅛in by 72in (129.9cm by 182.9cm)
New York $330,000 (£218,543). 20.V.86

Jacob Hendrik Pierneef
LANDSCAPE, NORTHERN TRANSVAAL
Signed and dated '49, $29\frac{7}{8}$in by $40\frac{1}{8}$in (76cm by 102cm)
Johannesburg R120,000 (£24,691:$35,555). 19.XI.85
From the collection of the F. H. Moerdyk family

Opposite
Frederick McCubbin
FEEDING TIME
Signed and dated *1893*, $29\frac{1}{8}$in by $49\frac{1}{4}$in (74cm by 125cm)
Melbourne Aus$693,000 (£333,173:$523,082). 21.IV.86

Sir Arthur Ernest Streeton
SUMMER DROVING
Signed and dated *1891*, $11\frac{3}{4}$in by $23\frac{5}{8}$in (30cm by 60cm)
Melbourne Aus$440,000 (£211,538:$332,115). 21.IV.86

Prints

Lucas Cranach the Elder
CHRIST ON THE CROSS WITH THE VIRGIN AND SAINT JOHN
Hand-coloured woodcut with gold leaf, *circa* 1504, 8½in by 6in (21.7cm by 15.2cm)
London £47,300 ($74,734). 27.VI.86

William Blake
ENOCH
Modified lithograph probably printed in relief from a stone, on wove paper, *circa* 1808,
sheet size 8⅞in by 12½in (22.4cm by 31.6cm)
London £28,600 ($43,186). 10.XII.85

Henri Matisse
NU AU COUSSIN BLEU À CÔTÉ D'UNE CHEMINÉE
Lithograph on wove paper, signed in pencil, and inscribed *7/10 épr. d'artiste*, 1925,
proof aside from the edition of fifty, 25in by 18⅞in (63.5cm by 47.9cm)
New York $93,500 (£61,513). 15.V.86

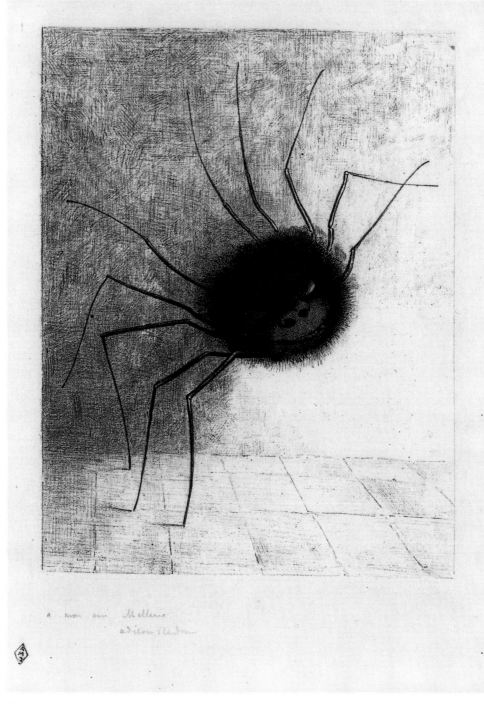

Odilon Redon
ARAIGNÉE
Lithograph on *chine appliqué* supported on wove paper, signed in pencil and
dedicated *à mon ami Mellerio*, inscribed *épreuve d'essai* on the support sheet, 1887,
proof before letters and edition of twenty-five, 11in by 8⅝in (28cm by 22cm)
London £52,800 ($83,424). 26.VI.86

Wassily Kandinsky
IN SOMMER
Woodcut printed in colours, inked in the manner of a
monotype, signed in white brushpoint on the support
sheet, 1904, sheet size 19⅝in by 11½in (49.8cm by 29.3cm)
New York $49,500 (£34,859). 15.XI.85

Maurice Prendergast
TELEGRAPH HILL
Monotype printed in colours on Japan paper laid on card, *circa* 1895, sheet size 14¾in by 15in
(37.4cm by 38cm)
New York $143,000 (£94,079). 15.V.86

Jasper Johns
GRAY ALPHABET
Lithograph printed in grey tones, signed in pencil, dated *1968* and numbered *55/59*, with the blindstamp of the publisher, 50¾in by 34in (129cm by 86.5cm)
New York $22,000 (£14,474). 16.V.86

Edvard Munch
MÄDCHEN AUF DER BRÜCKE
Woodcut and lithograph printed in five colours on wove paper, 1920, 19¾in by 16⅞in
(50.1cm by 43cm)
London £82,500 ($130,350). 26.VI.86

John James Audubon
CAROLINA PARROT
Hand-coloured engraving, Plate XXVI of *The Birds of America*, 1827–38,
33⅛in by 23¾in (84.2cm by 60.4cm)
New York $35,200 (£24,615). 18.X.85
From the collection of the New York City Department of Records and
Information Services

The complete set of four hundred and thirty-five engravings was sold for an
aggregate total of $1,761,842 (£1,232,057) for the benefit of the Municipal
Archives, Reference and Research Fund.

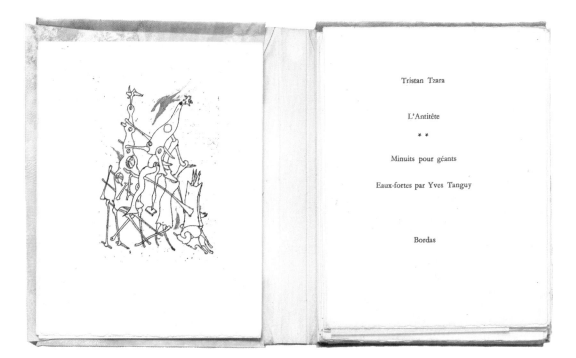

Tristan Tzara

L'ANTITÊTE, MONSIEUR AA, L'ANTIPHILOSOPHE, MINUITS POUR GÉANTS AND LE DESESPERANTO

Set of three volumes, numbered *19* of an edition of 31, with etchings by Max Ernst, Yves Tanguy and Joan Miró, including the cancelled copper plate for an etching by Yves Tanguy, published by Bordas, 1949, each sheet 5½in by 4½in (14cm by 11.5cm)

New York $26,400 (£18,592). 14.XI.85

Toulouse-Lautrec: poster designer

Richard Thomson

Toulouse-Lautrec's reputation rests, as he himself would have wished, not only on his work as painter and draughtsman but also on his oeuvre as a printmaker, above all on his remarkable colour lithographs and posters. For admirers of his prints 1985 was the *annus mirabilis*. It saw the publication of Wolfgang Wittrock's two-volume catalogue raisonné of Lautrec's printed work as well as a major exhibition, *Henri de Toulouse-Lautrec*, staged by the Museum of Modern Art in New York. His prints, and especially the posters, have also had a lively presence at auction, symptomatic not only of our appreciation for his work, but also of the lasting impact of his images.

A poster must be striking. It must convey information, too, but this function is greatly facilitated by an image that is immediately arresting. Lautrec was perhaps the earliest artist who consistently generated motifs that were at once potent and economical. Born in 1864, he belonged to the first generation that grew up attuned to a sophisticated world of mass consumption, to department stores and illustrated magazines, to seaside holidays and internationally popular forms of show business. His work in Paris as a poster designer was thus a necessary fusion of the artist's sense of design and technical virtuosity with the commercial realities of modern life.

In his first poster, *Moulin Rouge – La Goulue* (Fig. 1), published in 1891, Lautrec achieved this combination, drawing on his five years' previous experience painting dance-hall subjects. He knew the performers and the atmosphere of these establishments well, and had a repertoire of motifs ready to be refined into a poster design. In simplified silhouettes, Lautrec described the public of the Moulin Rouge, the fine women of uncertain status, the gentlemen 'slumming it', without detracting from the central star. La Goulue was at the height of her career in 1891, her renown based on the energetic salacity of her dance, a version of the can-can that made much of indelicate gestures and frothing petticoats, low cleavages and high kicks. Lautrec's tellingly outlined crowd, wierdly detached partner and promiscuously posed Goulue encapsulated the risqué delights of the Moulin Rouge.

The succeeding years saw Lautrec produce a sequence of equally effective images. His poster for *Jane Avril* made in 1893, focused once more on the performer herself, famed for her strange can-can. Lautrec set Jane's gangling figure, self-absorbed in her dance, against the thrusting male presence of the double bass, once again implying the nature of her performance within the immediate impact of his design.

Fig. 1
Henri de Toulouse-Lautrec
MOULIN ROUGE (LA GOULUE)
Lithograph printed in colours on two joined sheets, 1891, sheet size $67\frac{1}{8}$in by $48\frac{1}{4}$in
(170.5cm by 122.5cm)
New York $38,500 (£27,113). 16.XI.85

The *Divan Japonais* of the same year saw an even subtler approach. It is an advertisement for a particular café-concert, not a specific star. Both the performer, Yvette Guilbert, and the conductor of the orchestra, who would conventionally have expected to be emphasised, remain unidentified; the quality of performance at the Divan Japonais is assumed: a sophisticated marketing device. Rather, Lautrec stressed the audience. Using his friends Jane Avril and Édouard Dujardin as models, placing them ambiguously so that we are uncertain whether they are together or if the man is about to approach the woman, he implied that this café-concert's public was chic while simultaneously suggesting that it was licentious: an effective and inviting combination.

By mid-decade Lautrec was well established as both printmaker and poster designer, and his horizons widened. He began to mix with and work for the sophisticated circle of *La Revue Blanche*, the most influential literary and artistic periodical of the Belle Epoque. Lautrec chose one of the proprietors' wives, Misia Natanson, an accomplished pianist and society hostess, to embody the spirit of the review for his poster of 1895. He chose to represent her skating, the then fashionable pastime and a far cry from the coarse world of popular entertainment.

Lautrec was also involved with another periodical, *La Plume*, producing *La Passagère du 54* to advertise their poster exhibition of 1896, in which he exhibited *Elles*, his great suite of colour lithographs. The clowness Cha-u-Kao who worked, as far as we know, as both clown and prostitute, appears with her lesbian lover as the main protagonist of the series. With *Elles* Lautrec was at the summit of his virtuosity as a lithographer, his line decisive and vivacious, his skill with techniques like spatter under total control, and his colour at once subtle and resplendent.

But as the 1890s wore to a close, and as Lautrec's twin problems of syphilis and alcoholism grew critical and then hopeless, the quality of his work inevitably suffered. His penultimate poster, executed in 1899 and again of *Jane Avril* (Fig. 2), is indicative of these difficulties. Gone are the delicate colour effects, the economical insertion of information, to be replaced by stark contrasts and blunt lettering. Nevertheless, the poster has an eerie, hypnotic quality, as the patterned serpent on her dress seems to wind up her swaying body. The poster was never used.

Toulouse-Lautrec was one of the most important printmakers of his rich and innovative period. Appreciation of his work is undiminished. We relish just as much today the vitality of his drawing, the strength and the subtlety of his colour, and the impact of his images; qualities often best combined in his magisterial posters. His stock has never been higher.

Fig. 2, *opposite*
Henri de Toulouse-Lautrec
JANE AVRIL
Lithograph printed in colours on wove paper, signed in pencil, from the edition of twenty-five, 1899, sheet size 22in by 15in (56cm by 38.1cm)
New York $60,500 (£42,606). 16.XI.85

Photographs

Maurice Guibert
HENRI DE TOULOUSE-LAUTREC IN
JAPANESE SAMURAI DRESS
One of two gelatin silver and albumen
prints, one signed and inscribed in pencil
on the mount, *circa* 1892, 6in by 3¾in
(15.2cm by 9.5cm)
New York $20,900 (£13,571). 12.V.86

Alfred Stieglitz
SUN RAYS−PAULA−BERLIN
Silver print, signed and inscribed in
pencil on the mount *For Edward Dahlberg*,
circa 1889, 9in by 6⅝in
(22.9cm by 16.8cm)
New York $42,900 (£30,426). 12.XI.85
From the collection of Mr and
Mrs Alan Koppel

Edward Steichen

BALZAC, THE OPEN SKY, 11 P.M.
Olive-green pigment print, signed and dated
MDCCCCVIII with a stylus on the image,
19¾in by 14⅞in (50.2cm by 37.8cm)
New York $53,900 (£35,000). 12.V.86

This photograph is one of a series by Steichen of
Rodin's *Balzac*.

Paul Strand

YOUNG BOY, GONDEVILLE, FRANCE
Silver print, 1951, 4⅝in by 5¾in
(11.8cm by 14.6cm)
New York $38,500 (£25,000). 12.V.86

Bill Burnside
MARILYN MONROE
Silver print, inscribed in ink *To Bill, Anything worth having is worth waiting for! Love, Marilyn,*
circa 1950, 10¼in by 13¼in (26cm by 33.5cm)
London £17,600 ($28,160). 25.IV.86

David Bailey
BOB GELDOF
Silver print, signed by Bailey and Geldof, 1985,
20in by 16in (50.8cm by 40.7cm)
London £3,200 ($4,560). 4.XI.85

Members of the Photographic Club
ALBUM FOR THE YEAR 1855
Forty-one of the original forty-four photographs,
each plate titled and bearing details of the
photographic technique, printed by Charles
Whittingham
London £16,500 ($24,750). 1.XI.85

The photograph illustrated below is
*The Hippopotamus at the Zoological Gardens,
Regents Park,* by Count de Montizon.

The Gospels of St Hubert

Rosamond McKitterick

Gospel Books, containing the text of Matthew, Mark, Luke and John and the synoptic tables of Eusebius were the greatest treasures of the churches and monasteries and a few wealthy lay patrons in the early middle ages. Lavishly decorated, written on the finest parchment and painted in the most accomplished, and richest, scriptoria or writing centres of early medieval Europe, they were a manifestation of wealth and expensive taste, revered as holy objects, encased in magnificent bindings and kept on the altars of the churches. For a Carolingian Gospel Book (Fig. 1) to come onto the market is a rare event indeed. That it should be one of such major artistic and historical interest enhances its importance; for it is not a Gospel Book from an unknown writing centre and kept in an obscure and forgotten church, but one from the chief centre of the Franco-Saxon school of illumination in the Carolingian period, and a royal gift.

St-Amand, the main atelier for the Franco-Saxon style, produced a group of fine liturgical books on commission in the second half of the ninth century. Unlike the more lavish, even gaudy, products of such ateliers under royal patronage as Tours, Metz or Rheims, or the palace school of Charles the Bald, king of the west Franks (840–877), the Franco-Saxon style is more austere; it contains no human figures, leafy borders or purple pages, but is instead strictly decorative in a manner reminiscent of insular decoration, with delicate and intricate interlace and animal ornament. The commissioner of the St Hubert Gospels was evidently a man of discernment and impeccable taste. He appreciated the impact of fine lettering and elegant layout and the simple splendour of the decoration, in which the restrained use of gold and silver with masterly touches of green, yellow and red in the canon table pages, and the full-page illuminated capitals enhanced and complemented the delicate intricacy of the ornament.

The Gospel texts were written by one main hand throughout in an accomplished and elegant Caroline minuscule, with titles, headings and opening lines in graceful capitals and uncial script. An expert scribe corrected the text and made various alterations: one or two other hands can be detected in small sections of the text here and there. The corrector of the St Hubert Gospels can possibly be identified with the scribe of the splendid Sacramentary in New York (Pierpont Morgan G 57). The decoration is similar to that in Paris Bibliothèque Nationale lat. 257, Cologne

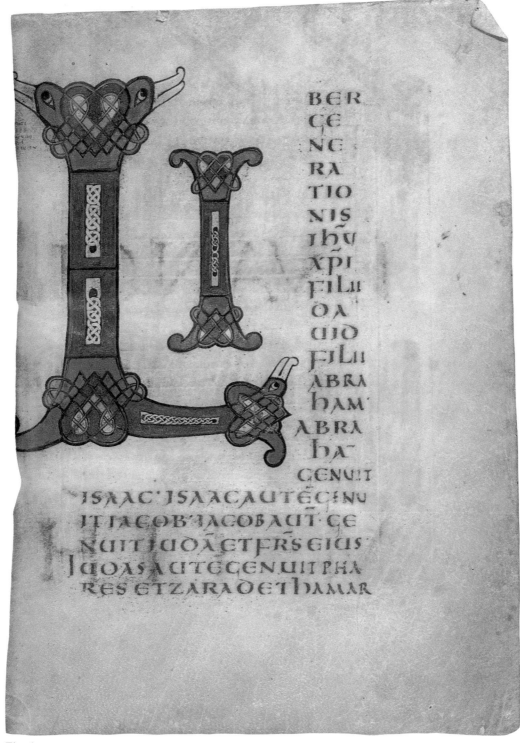

Fig. 1
The Gospels of St Hubert, an initial from St Matthew's Gospel, one of twenty full-page decorations
from an illuminated manuscript on vellum, Abbey of St-Amand, south Flanders, *circa* 879–82
London £1,430,000 ($2,187,900). 26.XI.85

Dombibliothek HS 14 and Paris Bibliothèque Nationale lat. 11956. Above all, Tours Bibliothèque Municipale MS 23 (Fig. 2) has the same array of what can only be Viking warriors in horned helmets forming the canon table columns. Bolder in this manuscript, the artist added toes to the Vikings' bare feet whereas in the St Hubert Gospel Book he left their socks on. The scribes and artists of these manuscripts were clearly contemporaries, working in the period 860–80, and trained in the same scriptorium. The high standards of their atelier were maintained in the layout and careful planning of the St Hubert Gospel Book. Even the leaves, once ruled on the hair side of the bifolium, were rearranged so that grooved hair-side faced grooved hair-side, and ridged flesh-side faced ridged flesh-side on each opening and thus presented the eye with no unsightly contrasts as the leaves of the book were turned.

There can be no doubt about the origin of this superb manuscript at the royal abbey of St-Amand, patronised by Charles the Bald, a grandson of Charlemagne himself. How the manuscript came to St Hubert near Liège on the other hand (its presence there is attested from about 1100) is less easy to explain, but there are a few clues. An eighteenth-century inscription on f.11v states that the codex was a gift of the Emperor Louis the Pious (814–40) in 825; the twelfth-century chronicle of St Hubert describes Louis' visit to the abbey then and the gifts he made, among them a wonderful Gospel Book. While the date 825 is stylistically impossible for the St Hubert Gospels, and the association with Louis the Pious equally so, the identification of the codex with one of the gifts Louis made on his momentous visit could have been due to the manuscript having originally been associated with another, later, Carolingian ruler of the same name who had also been a benefactor of St Hubert.

The history of both St-Amand, the producer, and St Hubert, the recipient, of the book, is relevant here, for both houses were of high political standing. The abbot of St-Amand at the time the St Hubert Gospels were produced was Gauzlin, archchancellor of Charles the Bald (d.877) and of his grandson Louis III (d.882), abbot of Jumièges, Glanfeuil, St-Amand and St Germain-des-Prés, Bishop of Paris from 884 and a doughty warrior to boot; he was killed in the Viking siege of Paris in 886. It was Gauzlin who presided over and undoubtedly masterminded the golden age of St-Amand book production, and it was he who presented Charles the Bald with its finest work, the Second Bible of Charles the Bald (Paris, Bibliothèque Nationale lat.2) in about 870. It is tempting indeed to see in the Viking canon tables in the St Hubert and Tours Gospel Books the artist's sly allusion to Gauzlin's own capture and ransom by Vikings in 858.

But it is not with Charles the Bald and the simple gratitude, or proud munificence of a client to his patron that the St Hubert Gospel Book should be connected. The Gospels were, rather, a contribution to the complicated political manoeuvres of Gauzlin in the succession crisis brought about by the premature death of Charles the Bald's son Louis the Stammerer in 879. Gauzlin and his party, who wished both of Louis' sons to succeed him and divide the kingdom between them, called

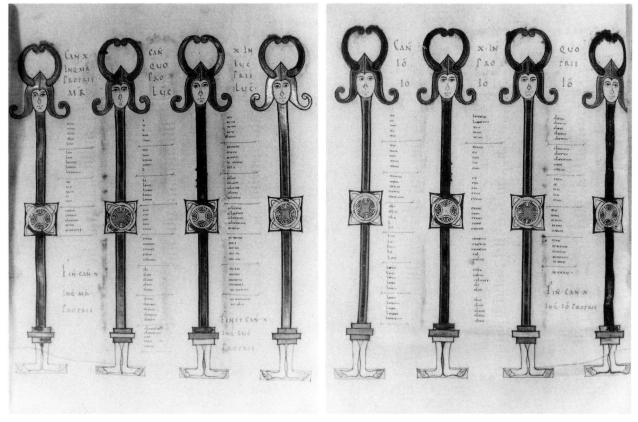

Fig. 2

Tours MS 23, folios 10r and 10v, two illuminated pages from the canon tables of a Gospel Book, second half ninth century

Reproduced courtesy of the Bibliothèque Municipale, Tours

on the assistance of their cousin, the east Frankish ruler Louis the Younger, to bring this about.

The monastery of St Hubert was in Louis the Younger's kingdom. It is thus very likely that the Gospel Book was part of the diplomatic gift, ordered by Gauzlin from his own scriptorium, to encourage Louis the Younger to render his assistance. It may subsequently have been given to the monastery of St Hubert by Louis before his death in 882, perhaps to offer up thanks to God for the definitive cession of territory to Louis made by the west Franks in 880. A much narrower chronology for the production of the St Hubert Gospel Book, 879–82, can therefore be proposed for this manuscript, in addition to establishing an important new historical context. With this interpretation, the Gospel Book of St Hubert represents a significant remnant of the political transformations and machinations of late Carolingian Europe and sheds new light on the personalities and institutions involved. Both as a witness to the beauty and superb quality of Carolingian book production, and as a vital piece of historical evidence, it is a great treasure.

Manuscripts

The opening of the Easter Mass, one of twenty-six separate vellum leaves
from a Latin Missal of Cistercian use, France or Spain, second half
twelfth century
London £7,700 ($11,781). 26.XI.85

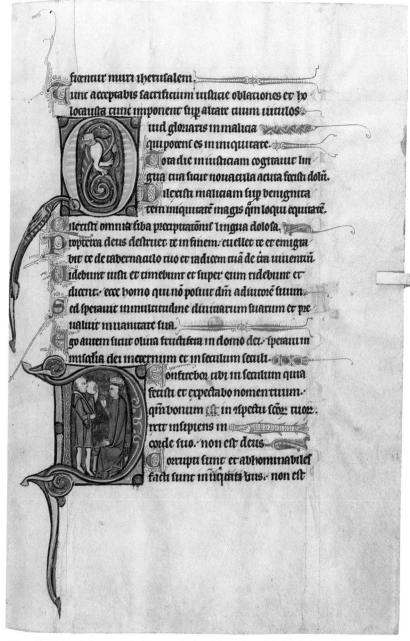

King David and the court fool, one of nine historiated initials in a Latin
Psalter illuminated in France for a German client, on vellum, Paris,
circa 1240
London £44,000 ($69,520). 24.VI.86
From the collection of the late Lionel Robinson, CBE, MC

Saint Gregory the Illuminator, one of three full-page miniatures in an illuminated manuscript of the Lives of the Saints, in Armenian, signed by the artist Mkrtich and the scribe Astuacatur, on paper, Tokad, 1679
London £24,200 ($37,026). 26.XI.85

All Saints, one of seventeen large miniatures in a manuscript Book of Hours illustrated in the workshop of the Boucicaut Master, and soon afterwards decorated with borders and Calendar miniatures in the workshop of the Rohan Master, in Latin and French, on vellum, Paris, *circa* 1415
London £572,000 ($903,760). 24.VI.86

Henry II sends into exile all Thomas Becket's relations, one of eight miniatures on four separate vellum leaves from an illustrated Life of Saint Thomas Becket in French verse, probably composed by Matthew Paris, St Albans or Westminster, second quarter thirteenth century London £1,375,000 ($2,172,500). 24.VI.86

The four leaves sold at Sotheby's on 24 June 1986, two of which are illustrated on these pages, were part of the only known medieval illustrated Life of Saint Thomas Becket, and are all that has survived of that unique work.

Thomas Becket arrives back in England, one of eight miniatures on four separate vellum leaves from an illustrated Life of Saint Thomas Becket in French verse, probably composed by Matthew Paris, St Albans or Westminster, second quarter thirteenth century
London £1,375,000 ($2,172,500). 24.VI.86

Qur'an, an Arabic manuscript in *naskhi* script, copied by Muhammad al-Imam, bound in
contemporary brown morocco tooled in blind and gold, Mamluk, *circa* 1400
London £46,200 ($73,458). 22.V.86

Krishna killing Sri Gala outside the kingdom of Karsapur, a page from the Mughal emperor
Akbar's copy of the Harivamsa, *circa* 1585–90
London £19,800 ($31,482). 22.V.86

Judaica

A German carved and painted wood circumcision ceremony box, late seventeenth century,
length 8in (20.2cm)
New York $33,000 (£22,603). 25.XI.85

A *Haggadah*, a Hebrew manuscript in Ashkenazi rabbinic square script and Hebrew cursive script, on vellum, copied by Yehuda Leib Ha'Cohen, Copenhagen, 1779
New York $165,000 (£113,014). 25.XI.85

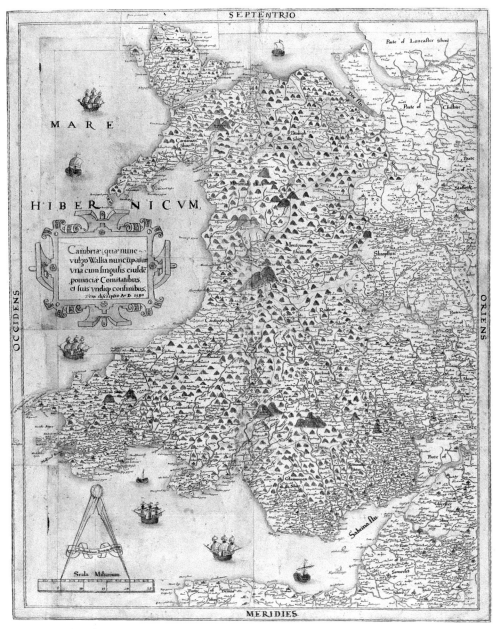

Christopher Saxton
Map of Wales, unrecorded working proof, two sheets joined, from a large wall-map of
England and Wales, *circa* 1580
London £66,000 ($104,940). 11.VII.86

This map is the first accurate delineation of Wales.

Opposite
Alonso de Molina
Vocabulario en la lengua Castellana y Mexicana, first edition, published by Juan Pablos,
Mexico, 1555
London £198,000 ($312,840). 26.VI.86
From the collection of the late Lionel Robinson CBE, MC

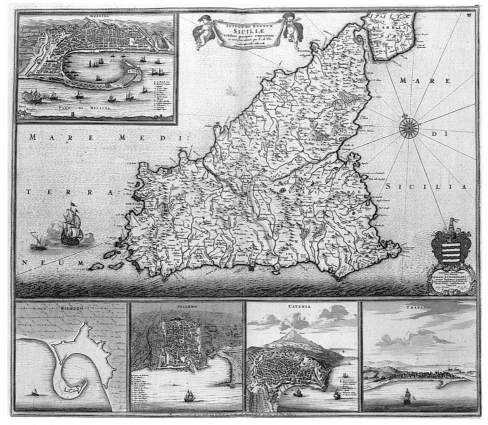

Frederick de Wit
Composite atlas with engraved
allegorical title, 128 maps and 26 sea
charts, Amsterdam, *circa* 1690
London £19,800 ($32,076). 8.V.86

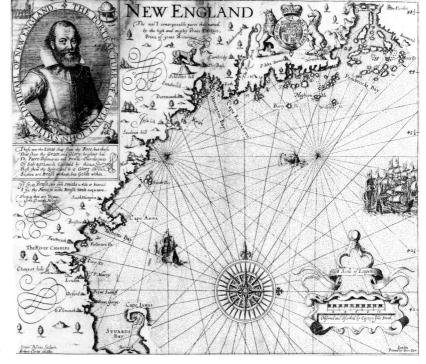

John Smith
A Description of New England, first
edition, with a folding engraved map
of New England, dedicated to the
Prince of Wales (later Charles I)
replaced from another copy, Humfrey
Lownes for Robert Clerke, London,
1616
New York $33,000 (£23,077). 31.X.85

Louis Claude Desaules de Freycinet
Baptism of Prime Minister Kalanimoku at Kawaihae, Hawaiian Islands from *Voyage autour du monde*,
four volumes, Paris, 1825–26
London £13,200 ($19,800). 7.XI.85

Paul Revere
A View of the Year 1765,
copperplate engraving, printed
by the engraver, Boston, 1776
New York $22,000 (£15,385)
31.X.85

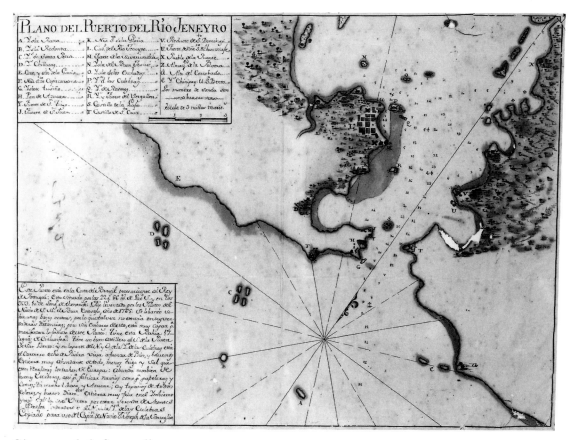

Giuseppe de la Somaglia
Seven manuscript diaries of naval voyages, 1748–78, over two thousand pages, twenty-one
manuscript naval charts and plans, *circa* 1770, and nine volumes of miscellany
New York $57,750 (£37,745). 23.IV.86

Opposite
Edward Lear
Illustrations of the Family of Psittacidae, or Parrots
42 hand-coloured lithographed plates, published by the author, 1832, bound with *A Monograph of
the Ramphastidae, or Family of Toucans*, Part I, by John Gould, 12 hand-coloured lithographed plates
by John and Elizabeth Gould and Edward Lear, published by the author, 1833
London £48,400 ($77,924). 9.V.86
From the collection of His Grace, The Duke of Northumberland KG, GCVO, TD, PC

MACROCERCUS ARARAUNA.

Blue & Yellow Maccaw

Ernest Shepard

Teddy Bear (the original Pooh Bear), one of the complete set of preliminary pencil drawings for A.A. Milne's *When We Were Very Young*, with the author's original pencil drafts for thirty-eight poems, the printer's working typescript, correspondence and copies of the book and other related publications, *circa* 1924
London £132,000 ($212,520)
10.VII.86
From the collection of
The Carl H. Pforzheimer Library

'Are you,' he said, 'by any chance
His majesty the King of France?'
The other answered, 'I am that,'
Bowed stiffly, and removed his hat;
Then said, 'Excuse me,' with an
air, 'But is it Mr. Edward Bear?'
And Teddy, bending very low,
Replied politely, 'Even so!'

Sir John Tenniel
Alice, a pencil and watercolour preparatory drawing for
Lewis Carroll's *Alice's Adventures in Wonderland*, 1864
London £37,400 ($59,092). 20.VI.86

Opposite
Edward Lear
A Book of Nonsense, two volumes, seventy-nine ink drawings with the accompanying
autograph manuscript verses, *circa* 1840
London £143,000 ($225,940). 20.VI.86

Head Quarters 18th. Octr. 1782

Sir,

I have been honored with two favors of your Excellency — One presented by the Count de Segur of the 2d. of April — the other delivered by the Prince de Broglio, of the 8th. — both wch. were rendered doubly agreeable, by the pleasure I had in receiving them from the hands of two such amiable young Gentlemen. —

Independent of my esteem for your Excellency — be assured Sir! that my respect & regard for the French Nation at large, to whom this Country is under so great obligations — as well as the very favourable Impressions I have conceived for these particular characters, will secure my warmest

attention

George Washington
Autograph letter to Benjamin Franklin, signed, three pages, 18 October 1782
New York $47,300 (£33,077). 31.X.85

John James Audubon
My Style of Drawing Birds, autograph manuscript essay, three pages, Edinburgh, 1831
New York $50,600 (£33,072). 23.IV.86

Franz Schubert
The autograph manuscript of the overture to
Fierabras, signed and inscribed by the composer,
sixty pages, 1823
London £165,000 ($260,700). 28.V.86

Karl Marx and Friedrich Engels
Manifest der Kommunistischen Partei, twenty-three
pages, first edition, second issue, J.E. Burghard,
London, 1848
London £26,400 ($41,712). 28.V.86

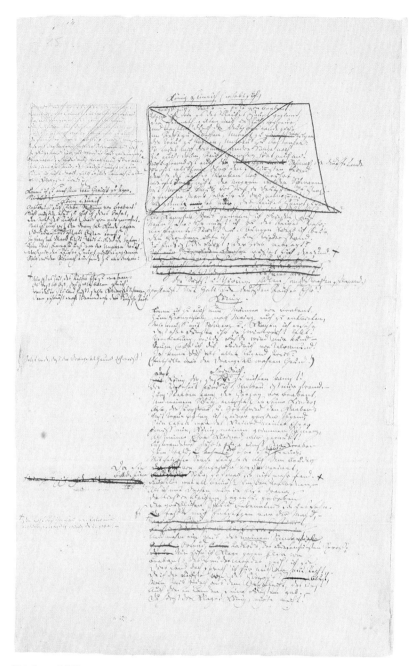

Richard Wagner
The autograph libretto of *Lohengrin*, unpublished first working draft,
twenty-nine pages, signed and dated *1845*
London £187,000 ($287,980). 29.XI.85

Above left

Charlotte Brontë

Autograph letter to Messrs Smith, Elder & Co, which accompanied the manuscript of *Jane Eyre*, signed *C Bell*, two pages, Haworth,
24 August 1847
London £27,500 ($41,388). 18.XII.85

Above right

The archive of John Lane

Aubrey Beardsley's autograph receipt detailing payments for *The Yellow Book*, 1894, one of the documents sold from the archive of John Lane, publisher at The Bodley Head, 1887–1921
London £187,000 ($281,435). 18.XII.85
From the collection of the Allen Lane Foundation

Left

Oscar Wilde

Autograph letter to Carlos Blacker, signed, twelve pages, Berneval-sur-Mer, 12 July 1897
London £22,000 ($35,420). 10.VII.86
From the collection of the Blacker family

Henry Miller
The Tropic of Cancer, original typescript, 926 pages, 1932–3
New York $165,000 (£113,793). 14.II.86
From the collection of Valentine Miller

D.H. Lawrence
Autograph manuscripts and typescripts of
Studies in Classic American Literature, circa 1920
New York $82,500 (£56,897). 14.II.86

Pierre-Joseph Redouté's *Les Liliacées*

Fanny Mallary

Occasionally a work of art comes onto the market which combines high quality, historical and artistic importance, illustrious provenance and sheer beauty. This was the case when Sotheby's in New York auctioned the original drawings for Pierre-Joseph Redouté's great flower book *Les Liliacées*. The 468 drawings on vellum, accompanied by a unique copy of the descriptive text printed on vellum, were inserted into sixteen huge green morocco albums, bound by Bozerian and Lefèbvre for the Empress Josephine, who had bought them from the artist. The drawings, which re-emerged after fifty years of virtual obscurity, delighted observers at exhibitions in New York and London. Miraculous for their accuracy, detail and luminosity of colour, the flowers seem to leap from the creamy vellum surface, inviting the onlooker to pluck them from the page. *Les Liliacées* is simply one of the greatest illustrated books ever produced. Although less famous than the same artist's *Les Roses*, which is the most often reproduced book in the history of botanical illustration, *Les Liliacées* is felt by many to surpass *Les Roses* in quality.

Pierre-Joseph Redouté was born in Saint Hubert in Belgium in 1759. Coming from a long line of painters, he entered the family business and spent his youth travelling round the Netherlands as a journeyman painter. At the age of twenty-three he arrived in Paris where he met the two men who shaped his career as a flower painter. The first was the eccentric French aristocrat Charles-Louis L'Héritier de Brutelle, a talented botanist who was working on a series of books on the exotic plants then being introduced into Europe. L'Héritier employed Redouté as an illustrator and taught him to make drawings that were botanically accurate. Redouté's second mentor was Gérard van Spaendonck, the great Dutch artist and professor of flower painting at the *Jardin du Roi*, who did much to hone Redouté's talents and further his career. Van Spaendonck hired Redouté to work on the *Vélins du Roi*, the national collection of natural history paintings begun by Louis XIV's uncle Gaston d'Orléans, and taught the young artist to paint with pure watercolour, rather than the traditional heavier gouache.

With his own extraordinary talent enhanced by the scientific knowledge of L'Héritier and the artistic influence of van Spaendonck, Redouté's reputation grew and he began his dazzling career as the 'Talleyrand of the arts'. Undaunted by the political upheavals of the age he became draughtsman to the cabinet of

Pierre-Joseph Redouté
Fig. 1, *Amaryllis brasiliensis*, one of 468 watercolour drawings on vellum from the
Empress Josephine's copy of *Les Liliacées*, all but sixty-five signed, the drawings and text
leaves inserted within the blank pages of sixteen folio volumes bound in contemporary
green morocco by Bozerian and Lefèbvre, 1802–1816, the drawings each approximately
19in by 13½in (48.3cm by 34.3cm)
New York $5,500,000 (£3,846,154). 20.XI.85

Marie-Antoinette, a prestigious but largely honorary position since the queen actually disliked painting. He subsequently became painter to the Empress Josephine and taught drawing to her successor, the Empress Marie-Louise. Under the restored Bourbons, Redouté was given a medal by Louis XVIII and the Légion d'honneur by Charles X, whose daughter-in-law the duchesse de Berry was his patroness. He taught drawing to the daughters of the duc d'Orléans and when their father became king, Redouté was appointed painter to Queen Marie-Amélie.

Redouté's most important patroness, however, was the Empress Josephine. As Napoleon rose to become First Consul of France and then Emperor, Josephine lavished huge sums on the gardens and decoration of the château at Malmaison, which she had acquired in 1798. Her contribution to botanical science was a real one. She had had a passion for flowers ever since her childhood in Martinique, and she used her husband's position to acquire exotic species for her garden. Many plants that are now commonplace in France were introduced through her efforts, and it has been estimated that as many as one hundred and eighty-four new species flowered in the gardens and hothouses of Malmaison. To assist her in her botanical pursuits she employed a number of distinguished botanists: to record the beauties of her gardens she hired Redouté.

During the period of his employment at Malmaison Redouté was at the height of his powers as a botanical artist and his major work of that period was *Les Liliacées*. Issued in parts between 1802 and 1816, the work comprised eight volumes containing a total of 486 plates, which illustrated not only plants of the family *liliaceae*, such as lily, asphodel, fritillaria, tulip, allium, hemerocallis etc. but also many other monocots, such as irises, amaryllis, agaves, commelinas. The work had particular scientific importance because this group of plants could not be preserved in herbaria, the collections of dried flowers used by botanists for protracted study. Through Redouté's work, the plants drawn with such remarkable detail and accuracy, a large number of species became available for examination. But, to the modern eye, more important than scientific considerations is the extraordinary beauty of the plates.

Although the Empress Josephine did not directly sponsor *Les Liliacées*, her patronage made it possible for Redouté to produce such an exquisite book. Through her influence Chaptal, Minister of the Interior, ordered eighty copies and these were given to the museums of France or as diplomatic gifts by the French government. The Empress also ordered several copies herself and bought the original drawings from Redouté for a sum variously estimated at 84,000 or 25,000 francs.

After Josephine's death the drawings passed to her son, Eugène de Beauharnais. They remained at Seeon in Bavaria, the seat of his family, the Dukes of Leuchtenburg, throughout the nineteenth century. At some point before 1890, some of the original drawings were removed from the set (their whereabouts is unknown) and the remaining 468, in their bindings, were sold at auction in Zurich in 1935. They were subsequently acquired by the New York art dealer Erhard Weyhe but disappeared from view until consigned for sale at Sotheby's in November 1985 by an anonymous trust.

Fig. 2, *above left*
Pancratium calathiforme, signed

Fig. 3, *above right*
Iris fimbriata, signed

Fig. 4, *right*
Tulipa gesneriana var. luteo-rubra

Coins
and medals

The Second World War Victoria
Cross group awarded to Leading
Seaman James Joseph Magennis,
H.M. Midget Submarine *XE.111*
London £31,900 ($51,359)
3.VII.86

Leading Seaman James Joseph
Magennis won the VC for showing
very great courage when he laid
limpet mines on the hull of the
Japanese cruiser *Takao* at Johore
Strait, 31 July 1945.

The Victoria Cross group awarded to Field-Marshal Sir George White, VC, GCB, OM, GCSI, GCMG,
GCIE, GCVO
London £60,500 ($91,355). 6.III.86

Sir George won the VC for conspicuous bravery during the Afghanistan Campaign. On 6 October
1879, at the Battle of Charasia, finding that the artillery and rifle fire failed to dislodge the enemy
from a fortified hill which it was necessary to capture, and that his men were exhausted and greatly
outnumbered, he alone advanced on the enemy and shot their leader. This act so intimidated the
enemy that they fled round the side of the hill, and the position was taken. Again on 1 September
1880, at the Battle of Kandahar, when leading the charge under heavy fire from the enemy, he rode
straight up to them, and secured one of their two guns, immediately after which the enemy retired.

The Nobel Peace Prize, gold medal awarded to Sir William Randal Cremer, 1903
London £11,550 ($17,441). 22.XI.85

Islamic, Umayyad dinar, AH 132
(AD 749)
Dubai $18,700 (£12,635). 4.XII.85

Islamic, Buwayhid dinar of
al-Marzuban, 'Uman, AH 385 (AD 995)
Dubai $12,650 (£8,547). 4.XII.85

England, pattern
quarter-sovereign of
Edward VI, *circa* 1550
London
£5,500 ($8,140). 13.II.86

Austria, 30 ducats struck in gold of
Leopold I, 1678
London £33,000 ($49,830). 22.XI.85

England, hammered
sixpence of Charles II,
circa 1660
London
£1,210 ($1,791). 13.II.86

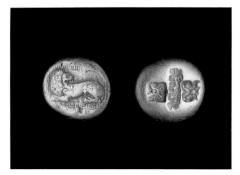

Anglo-Saxon, penny of Edward the
Elder (899–924)
London £2,420 ($3,582). 13.II.86

France, Ange d'or of
Philippe VI, 1342
Geneva SF25,300
(£7,857:$11,629). 11.XI.85

Ancient Greece,
Ionia, electrum stater of Miletus,
circa 575 BC
London £16,500 ($26,400). 20.V.86

Italy, Padua, silver medal by Giovanni
da Cavino depicting the Roman Empress
Faustina Junior, mid sixteenth century
London £1,430 ($2,145). 24.X.85
From the Virgil M. Brand Collection

Japan, 10 yen, Meiji year 4 (1871)
London £3,520 ($5,526). 21.VII.86

Ceylon, pattern
copper piece, *circa* 1802
London
£1,650 ($2,442). 13.II.86

Scotland, rider of James III
(1460–1488)
London £2,640 ($3,907). 13.II.86

Australia, sovereign of Queen
Victoria, 1855
London £6,160 ($9,117). 13.II.86

Great Britain, an early trial printing of the Treasury £1 note, prepared at the
outbreak of war, August 1914
London £1,650 ($2,492). 22.XI.85

South Africa, Orange River Colony, Boer War emergency £5 note, issued during the
siege of Koffyfontein, 1900
London £770 ($1,209). 17.VII.86

The Littlecote Armoury

Guy M. Wilson

In the autumn of 1985, the armoury of Littlecote House in Wiltshire came on the market together with the other contents of the house. The disposal and consequent dispersal of collections of important objects is not, of course, uncommon, but the Littlecote armoury is one of those few collections which is important simply because as a collection it is unique. The arms and armour of which it consists are of the type that were standard issue during those troubled years in the middle of the seventeenth century when Englishman fought Englishman over a complex of political, religious and social issues. It has been displayed ever since on the walls of Littlecote House as a memorial for those who gave their lives for what they believed was right. In this sense it is very much a part of our national heritage, and it was therefore appropriate that through the generosity of many, including the Department of the Environment, the National Heritage Memorial Fund, the Esmée Fairbairn Charitable Trust and J. Paul Getty, Jr, and many thousands of other donors, the Royal Armouries were able to acquire the Littlecote armoury intact.

At the time of the English Civil War the Littlecote estate was owned by the Popham family who had acquired it in 1589. Sir Francis Popham died in 1644 and it was his surviving sons, Alexander (Fig. 1), Hugh and Edward who took an active part in the conflicts of the time on the side of Parliament. What remains at Littlecote today are surviving pieces from the arms and equipment acquired by the Popham brothers to equip the forces they raised during those turbulent years, to which various other pieces have been added more recently to improve the displays.

The surviving armoury consists principally of the armours and equipment of a force of harquebusiers, or light cavalry, including breasts, backs, pot helmets, buff coats, leather cross-belts, carbines and pistols. These are still sufficient to equip more than thirty troopers. The majority of the cuirasses (breasts and backs) appear to date from the Commonwealth period (1649–60) for they are stamped with the Commonwealth mark, the cross of St George, and with the helmeted, rather than crowned, 'A' that the Armourers' Company of London adopted at this period. The backs and breasts at least, therefore, appear to be of equipment issued after the fighting was over, but nevertheless at a time when large numbers of troops were kept under arms to keep the peace and prevent the disaffected from causing further unrest. All the pot helmets, which appear to come from the historic armoury, are of the English type, with a three-bar face-guard attached to the pivoting brim.

Fig. 1
English school
EQUESTRIAN PORTRAIT OF GENERAL ALEXANDER POPHAM
Inscribed, *circa* 1667, 90in by 90in (228cm by 228cm)
Littlecote House 21.XI.85

This painting was sold by private treaty to HM Tower of London

The buff coats are exceptionally well preserved, retaining a bright yellow colour; some are marked with initials, presumably of the soldiers to whom they were issued; some retain the original linings for trunk and arms; some have their original laces; and one shows clearly how the coats were fastened at the front, not by the laces, which were purely decorative, but by internal iron hooks and eyes.

Accompanying these harquebusiers' armours, and displayed with them for many years, are a number of shoulder pieces or pauldrons from heavy cavalry or cuirassier armours. None of the swords which would have been used with these harquebusiers' armours survives, but more than sixty pistols and nearly twenty carbines remain at Littlecote. Many of the firearms have been extensively repaired, and a number completely re-stocked. All the pistols which can be ascribed to the historic armoury with some confidence are conventional mid-seventeenth-century full stocked holster pistols with flint-locks of the type which are generally referred to as English locks, although close examination has shown that they vary quite considerably both internally and externally, and that they may be divided into three distinct types. Some have lock-plates of wheel-lock form and some have lock-plates of brass. Some are signed by the gunmaker Robert Murden, who is recorded as producing military firearms during the English Civil Wars, and twenty-three bear the marks of the Gunmakers' Company of London. Some have branded into their stocks the initials *A.P.*, presumably those of Alexander Popham the commander of the cavalry unit to which they were issued. Thirteen of the carbines are almost identical, and are probably the only carbines to survive from the original armoury. They are characterised by large barrels with a large calibre (.82 in.) and bellied muzzles, and full stocks with very distinctive deep-bellied flat-sided butts on which are carved stylised dragon's heads. It is an intriguing thought that the use of these 'dragon' guns might be the origin of the term dragoon!

This then was the equipment of the ordinary cavalry trooper. However, the armoury also contains a vastly superior set of equipment, which has always been thought to be that of the commander, Alexander Popham, himself. It consists of a fine, short buff coat with double sleeves and double collar, a pair of buff gauntlets, and a heavy cuirass of the best quality with decorative straps and hooks which suggest that it may have been made in the Royal Armour Workshop at Greenwich. A superior quality three-bar pot helmet in the armoury may belong to this armour. It has a one-piece, rather than two-piece skull and a transverse scroll bar joining the three vertical bars of the face-guard. Associated with this armour is a fine horseman's sword with a gilt hilt, which may also have belonged to Alexander Popham.

As well as the mass of cavalry equipment, the Littlecote armoury also contains some of the equipment of an infantry regiment, perhaps of that regiment which Alexander Popham raised in 1642, or more likely of the forces he raised after the disaster at Roundway Down in 1643. In addition there are a number of pikeman's armours, but there is good reason to believe that they have been associated in recent years. What are undoubtedly part of the historic armoury are the collection of more than eighty muskets. Approximately half are equipped with

Fig. 2
A view of the Littlecote armoury displayed in the Great Hall at Littlecote House.

matchlocks and half with flintlocks, and these two groups both consist of roughly equal numbers of weapons with 'fishtail' and 'club' butts. Many of the flintlock muskets show signs of conversion from matchlock. As with the pistols and carbines all the flintlocks are of the form commonly referred to as 'English locks', although detailed inspection has revealed that they can be divided into four distinct groups. Sixteen of the muskets have barrels stamped with the proof-mark of the Gunmakers' Company of London, and two, very interestingly, are stamped with the Liège 'perron' mark, indicating that they were imported from Belgium. A number of the muskets, like the pistols, are branded with the initials of Alexander Popham.

Much more research needs to be carried out before all the questions surrounding the armoury can be answered. There is no doubt, however, of the value of the collection, which has preserved large numbers of the armours and weapons used by the ordinary soldiers of the time, just the sort of equipment which does not often survive. Happily, now the armoury has been secured for the nation by the Royal Armouries it will be available for view and study by future generations, assured of proper care, preservation and interpretation.

Arms and armour

A gold-mounted Greek sword with a gold-mounted leather scabbard, *circa* 1812
London £8,800 ($14,168). 15.V.86

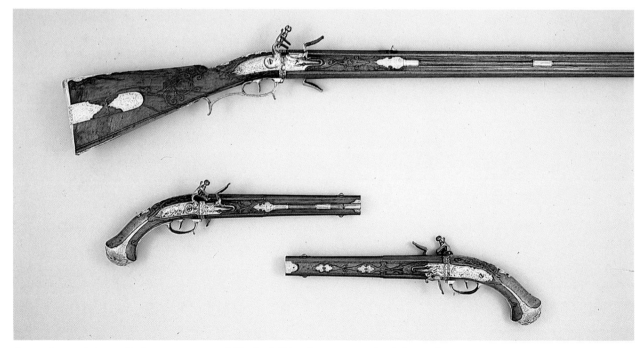

A garniture of three gilt-bronze-mounted flintlock Wender arms, early eighteenth century
London £22,000 ($35,420). 15.V.86
From the collection of the late Charles De Pauw

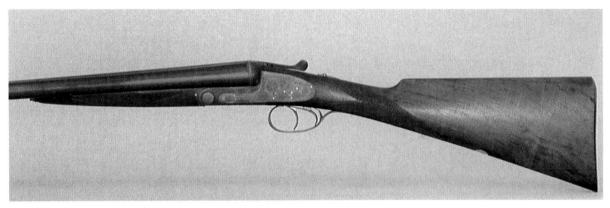

A pair of 12-bore self-opening round-bodied sidelock ejector guns by Boss & Co., 1939
Billingshurst £15,400 ($23,870). 12.III.86

The game records of Lord Ripon, comprising fifty-three leather-bound volumes, 1871–1923,
fourteen cloth-bound pocket notebooks, dating from 1865 and later, and thirty game cards
£48,400 ($75,020)
A 12-bore hammer non-ejector gun by J. Purdey & Sons, number two of a set of three built for
Lord Ripon in 1890
£6,600 ($10,230)

The game records and gun illustrated above are from the collection of H. Vyner and were sold at
Billingshurst on 12 March 1986.

Works of art

A Florentine glazed terracotta relief of the Virgin and Child, workshop of Giovanni della Robbia, *circa* 1515, height 26½in (67.3cm)
New York $26,400 (£18,082). 22.XI.85

A bronze relief of the *Ecce Homo*, mid sixteenth century, height 13¾in (35cm)
London £107,800 ($160,622). 12.XII.85

A bronze group of Mercury and Cupid, seventeenth century, height 31½in (80cm) London £291,500 ($434,335). 12.XII.85

A south German bronze figure of
Orpheus, probably Augsburg, last
quarter sixteenth century,
height 12¾in (32.5cm)
New York $74,250 (£50,510). 31.V.86
From the collection of David M. Daniels

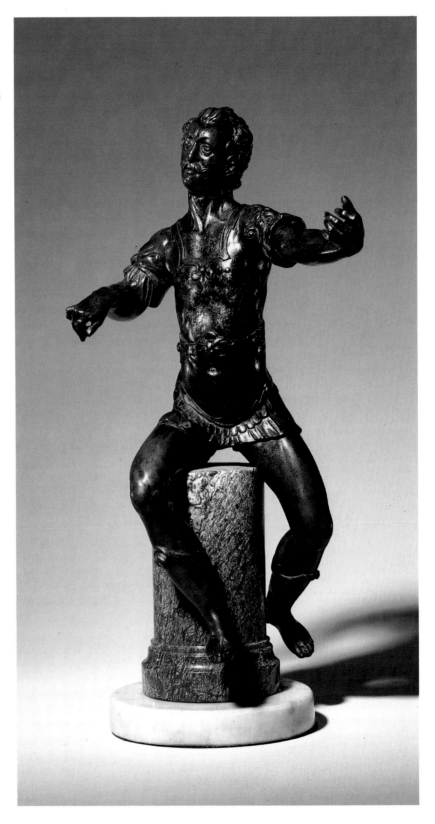

A Venetian marble figure of Meleager by
Antonio Gai, signed and dated 1735,
height 56¼in (143cm)
London £71,500 ($112,255). 22.IV.86

Opposite
A bronze bust of a young man attributed
to Pier Jacopo Alari-Bonacolsi, called Antico,
Mantua, first quarter sixteenth century,
height 28in (71cm)
Monte Carlo FF5,550,000 (£538,835:$786,119)
23.II.86
From the collection of the Duc de Talleyrand-
Périgord

A pair of Baroque gilt oak angels, probably Austrian, *circa* 1680, height 38½in and 39½in (97.8cm by 100.3cm)
New York $45,100 (£30,680). 31.V.86
From the collection of Constance and the late Edgar P. Richardson

An English carved limewood coronation relief of Queen Anne, workshop
of Grinling Gibbons, *circa* 1702, height 42½in (108cm)
London £20,900 ($33,649). 3.VII.86
From the Rous Lench Collection

The Dowager Empress inspecting the troops at Krasnoe Selo, one of a collection of personal photographs in an album assembled by Grand Duchess Xenia Alexandrovna, 1904–1905, 17¼in by 13¾in (44cm by 35cm)
London £30,800 ($45,584). 13.II.86

The Grand Duchess Xenia Alexandrovna lived from 1875 until 1960. She was the fourth child of Emperor Alexander III and sister of Nicholas II. She married her cousin Grand Duke Alexander Mikhailovich.

A Fabergé enamel miniature frame, workmaster H. Wigström, St Petersburg, *circa* 1916,
height 7⅜in (18.8cm)
London £27,500 ($40,975). 28.X.85
From the collection of the late John Sheldon

A Birmingham japanned casket containing two enamel tea caddies and a sugar canister, *circa* 1760, width 9½in (24cm)
London £28,600 ($42,900). 22.X.85

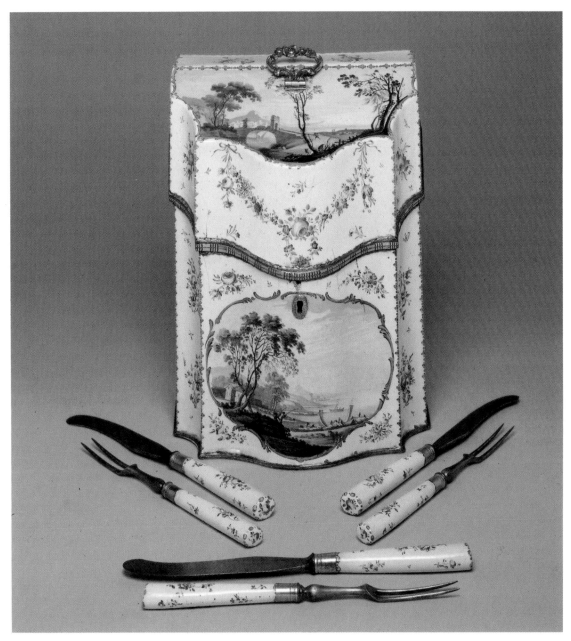

A Staffordshire knife case, *circa* 1765, height 10in (25.5cm)
London £34,100 ($55,242). 7.VII.86
From the Rous Lench Collection

A German gold and mother-of-pearl snuff box, mid eighteenth century,
width 3⅜in (8.5cm)
London £23,100 ($34,419). 28.X.85
From the collection of the late John Sheldon

A jewelled gold and enamel double musical box by Jean-George Rémond & Cie,
Geneva, *circa* 1810, width 3½in (9cm)
Geneva SF82,500 (£25,700:$38,037). 14.XI.85

Above, left to right
A jewelled gold and enamel snuff box in
the form of a peach, Geneva, *circa* 1800,
width 2⅜in (6cm), £13,750 ($20,488)
A Swiss pearl-set gold and enamel
vinaigrette, maker's mark of Moulinié
Bautte & Cie, early nineteenth century,
width 1½in (3.8cm), £5,500 ($8,195)
A jewelled gold and enamel snuff box,
maker's mark of Bessière & Schneider,
Geneva, *circa* 1815, width 2⅜in (6cm)
£6,380 ($9,506)

Right
A jewelled gold and enamel automaton
watch and musical snuff box in the
form of a butterfly by Piguet et Meylan,
Geneva, *circa* 1810, width 3⅛in (8cm)
£83,600 ($124,564)

The objects illustrated on this page are from the collection of the late John Sheldon and were sold in
London on 28 October 1985.

A Habsburg gold and enamel presentation cup, Imperial Workshops, dated 1665,
height 6¾in (17.2cm)
New York $187,000 (£132,624). 11.XII.85
From the collection of Nelson A. Rockefeller

This cup was presented to the Holy Roman Emperor Leopold I by his Privy Counsellor Reichsgraf
Georg Nikolaus zu Rosenberg.

A Portuguese jewelled gold crown, mid eighteenth century, height 8¼in (21cm)
New York $165,000 (£117,021). 11.XII.85
From the collection of Nelson A. Rockefeller

A Russian icon of the Dormition of the Virgin and another of the Anastasis, attributed to Ivan
Sobol, late sixteenth century, $8\frac{5}{8}$in by $6\frac{3}{4}$in (22cm by 17cm)
London each panel £8,800 ($13,024). 14.XI.85

A Cretan triptych on the theme of the Last Judgement by George Klontzas, signed, late sixteenth
century, excluding frame 10in by 24in (25.5cm by 61cm)
London £79,200 ($117,216). 14.XI.85

George, the son of Andrew Klontzas, belonged to a well known family of artists, and is ranked
amongst the greatest masters of Cretan painting of the late sixteenth century. The miniature scale
of representation in his icons is highly individual.

The Clore miniatures

Graham Reynolds

British collectors, on the whole, have cast a lack-lustre eye on Continental portrait miniatures. The national school has been so strong, varied and continuous over four centuries that it has seemed unnecessary to look for quality beyond our shores. In England only the Wallace Collection, formed by Francophiles living in Paris, can profess to show anything resembling a representative group of miniatures from the European masters.

The appearance in the March salerooms of the first portion of the Clore collection of portrait miniatures suggested that this neglect has been short-sighted, and has resulted in a failure to acquire examples which would add diversity and contrast to a purely British display. The history of the collection, which was richest in French miniatures, guaranteed its almost uniformly high quality. It had been brought together by the late David David-Weill, a connoisseur with a fine judgement and an enthusiasm for eighteenth-century French art. He amassed over 860 miniatures and when deciding on their ultimate disposal, called in a committee of experts to divide his collection into two sections of equal size and quality. He bequeathed one of these portions to the Musée du Louvre, which received them after David-Weill's death in 1952. The other half was acquired by Messrs Wildenstein and it was this moiety of the David-Weill collection that was bought by Sir Charles Clore. It is now being dispersed in two sessions, the first of which consisted of works by the artists whose names begin with the letters A – K.

At the outset miniature painting was carried out on vellum. A technical advance in the seventeenth century popularised the use of enamel and this led to the first flourishing of the Continental miniature, notably in the hands of Petitot and Bordier. Almost a third of the collection were enamels and here the English collector could feel at home. Amongst the most effective early works was the copy of Giordano's *Venus and Cupid* by Charles Boit (Fig. 1), which had belonged to the archetypal connoisseur of vertu, Horace Walpole.

The more fundamental change from vellum to ivory as a support, inaugurated by Rosalba Carriera at the beginning of the eighteenth century, allowed the Continental miniaturists a greater range of expression. Some European critics consider that the mid-eighteenth French painters made better use of the new material than their English contemporaries, Meyer, Cosway and Smart, since they

Fig. 1
Charles Boit
Venus and Cupid, after Luca Giordano, signed,
circa 1700, 1⅞in (4.7cm)
London £3,300 ($5,049). 17.III.86

Fig. 2
Pierre Adolphe Hall
Louise Félicité Victoire d'Aumont,
Princesse de Monaco,
signed, *circa* 1782, 3⅛in (8cm)
London £46,200 ($70,686). 17.III.86

Fig. 3
Jean-Honoré Fragonard
A young boy, circa 1770, 2½in (6.4cm)
London £11,000 ($16,830). 17.III.86

The miniatures illustrated on this page are from the collection of the late Sir Charles Clore

Fig. 4
François Dumont
A lady, signed and dated *l'an 3me*, 3in (7.5cm)
London £7,920 ($12,118). 17.III.86

Fig. 5
François Dumont
A young lady as Sappho, circa 1790, 3⅞in (10cm)
London £34,100 ($52,173). 17.III.86

achieved an impastoed texture based on the contrast between gouache and water-colour, rather than depending on the linear hatching of British masters.

It was possible to test the justice of this judgement amongst the numerous works by Pierre Adolphe Hall in the sale, mostly from his later period (Fig. 2), when he had achieved ample breadth and combined transparent washes with a colourful array of ribbons, bows and roses, rendered in gouache. The culmination of this rococo style is found in the miniatures of Jean-Honoré Fragonard (Fig. 3), of which there were two examples in the Clore collection. With their diffused light, their liquid drawing and their broad smudges of pigment, they are 'all a-flutter like a lady's fan'. But even as they were being painted Neo-Classicism was beginning to erode the basis of this casual elegance. A new austerity became apparent in the approach of the next generation of miniaturists. It is a tribute to the refining influence of Stanislaus Leczinski, ex-King of Poland, that François Dumont, Jean-Baptiste-Jacques Augustin and Jean-Baptiste Isabey were all trained in the art schools he had set up in Lorraine. It fell to them to translate the stern attitudes of the Revolution into miniature portraiture with the conviction that we see, for instance, in Dumont's unknown lady dated *l'an 3me* (1795) (Fig. 4), which compares interestingly with his earlier miniature of *A young lady as Sappho* (Fig. 5).

One of the more accomplished exponents of the new manner was Marie-Gabrielle Capet. Her *Cartographer* (Fig. 6) directs a fixed gaze at the spectator and is lit in the same way as David's portraits, from above with a raking side light that casts

Fig. 6
Marie-Gabrielle Capet
A cartographer, circa 1795, 3½in (8.8cm)
London £50,600 ($77,418). 17.III.86

The miniatures illustrated on these pages are from the collection of the late
Sir Charles Clore

Fig. 7
Heinrich Friedrich Füger
Marie Clementine, Archduchess of Austria, signed and dated *1795*, 5⅞in (15cm)
London £47,300 ($72,369). 17.III.86

Fig. 8, *opposite*
Jean-Baptiste Isabey
Madame Feydeau, watercolour on paper, signed and dated *1823*, 5¼in (13.4cm)
London £12,100 ($18,513). 17.III.86

The miniatures illustrated on these pages are from the collection of the late Sir Charles Clore

pronounced shadows to emphasise the austere republican virtues of diligence and resolve. Yet, at the same time, in Austria, Heinrich Friedrich Füger had not abandoned the lessons he had learned from Hall, as his impressive portrait of *Marie Clementine, Archduchess of Austria* (Fig. 7) clearly demonstrates.

Along with the constant repetition of the imperial image, the advent of Napoleon brought a softening in the attitude of the painter to his subject. Isabey proceeded from the charm of his *Amie de M. Delessert, circa* 1805 to the frothy Romanticism of his *Madame Feydeau* (Fig. 8) of 1823, which anticipates the levity of her son's farces. Augustin had many English sitters after the Battle of Waterloo, and his later work shows evidence of an accommodation with early nineteenth-century British style.

The works in the Clore collection exemplify some movements in taste and history radically different from those experienced by English miniature painters. As was to have been expected, most of these miniatures are returning to Europe, whence they originated.

Richard Gibson
Sir Thomas Wolryche, on vellum, signed with initials, *circa* 1690, 3in (7.4cm)
London £10,450 ($16,511). 9.VI.86

Samuel Cooper
A young gentleman, *circa* 1660, 3¼in (8.2cm)
London £16,500 ($26,070). 9.VI.86
From the collection of Ernst Holzscheiter

Pierre Adolphe Hall
Prince Joseph Antoine Poniatowski, signed, *circa* 1770, 4⅜in (11cm)
Geneva SF60,500 (£20,370:$32,796). 15.V.86

Opposite, left to right
Jean-Baptiste Isabey
Count Charles Esterhazy, signed and dated *1818*, 4⅞in (12.5cm)
Geneva SF16,500 (£5,556:$8,944). 15.V.86

François Meuret
The Countess of Clermont-Tonnerre, signed and dated *1861*, 3⅞in (9.8cm)
London £7,700 ($12,166). 9.VI.86
From the collection of Ernst Holzscheiter

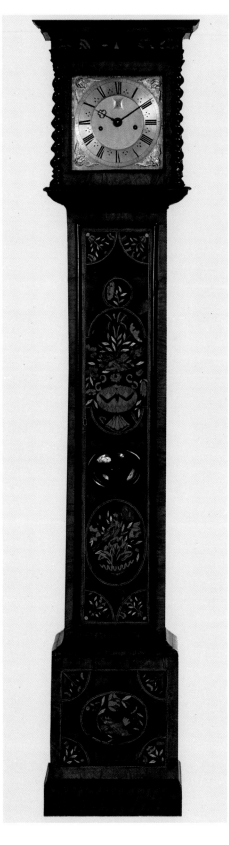

Clocks and watches

An olivewood, walnut and marquetry longcase clock,
signed *Johannes Knibb Oxoniae fecit, circa* 1680,
height 6ft 6in (198cm)
London £28,600 ($43,472). 20.II.86

An ebony-veneered quarter-repeating bracket timepiece by Thomas Tompion, No. 66,
circa 1685, height 12in (30.5cm)
London £41,800 ($64,790). 5.XII.85
From the collection of the late Sir John Prestige

Two similar gold and enamel heart-shaped
cylinder watches by James Cox, London, *circa*
1780, height *left* 2⅛in (5.5cm); *right* 2¼in (5.8cm)
Left London £13,200 ($19,668). 28.X.85
Right London £14,850 ($22,127). 28.X.85
From the collection of the late John Sheldon

A gold and enamel quarter-repeating musical watch
by Berthoud, Paris, No. 1707, *circa* 1820, with a
portrait miniature of Napoleon signed *Terroux P.*,
diameter 2¼in (5.8cm)
London £11,220 ($17,054). 20.II.86
From the collection of the late Sir Charles Clore

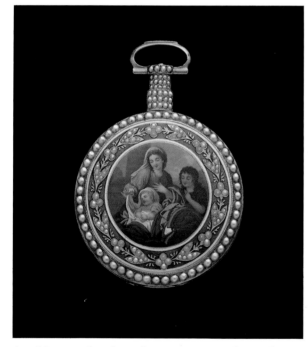

A gold, enamel and pearl-set sweep-seconds watch
for the Oriental market, by Ilbery, London,
No. 6658, *circa* 1800, diameter 2½in (6.2cm)
New York $33,000 (£23,077). 30.X.85

A gold and enamel musical automaton watch by
Louis Duchêne et Fils, Geneva, *circa* 1800,
diameter 2⅜in (6.1cm)
Geneva SF101,200 (£31,429:$46,514). 12.XI.85

A gold open face one-minute tourbillon by Patek Philippe, No. 198432, 1931, diameter 2in (5.1cm)
New York $99,000 (£66,000). 16.VI.86

A gold hunting cased five-minute-repeating watch by Patek Philippe, No. 47242, *circa* 1870, diameter $2\frac{1}{10}$ in (5.3cm)
New York $23,100 (£15,931). 15.II.86

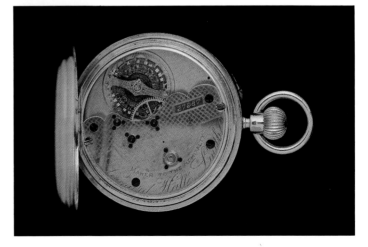

A gold open face six-minute tourbillon by Leonard Hall, Louth, No. 37987, 1890, diameter 2in (5.1cm)
New York $22,000 (£14,667). 16.VI.86

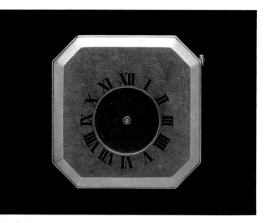

A platinum octagonal mystery watch by Cartier,
No. 5706, width 1⅝in (4.2cm)
New York $25,300 (£17,448). 15.II.86

A gold fusee keyless lever tourbillon by
Charles Frodsham, No. 19562/12172, 1912,
diameter 2⅜in (5.9cm)
London £23,100 ($35,112). 20.II.86

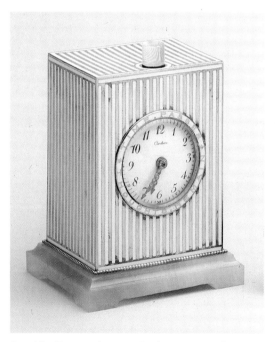

A gold, silver and enamel minute-repeating
desk clock by Cartier, the movement by
Nocturne, No. 2335, height 2⅞in (7.3cm)
London £11,550 ($17,210). 28.X.85
From the collection of the late John Sheldon

A gold minute-repeating perpetual calendar
keyless lever watch by Breguet, No. 1437,
circa 1925, diameter 1⅞in (4.8cm)
Geneva SF 35,200 (£10,932:$16,179). 12.XI.85

Top row, left to right
A minute-repeating wristwatch by Vacheron & Constantin, No. 341034, *circa* 1950,
diameter 1⅜in (3.6cm)
New York $22,000 (£15,172). 15.II.86
A gold chronograph wristwatch with perpetual calendar moon phases, tachometer and register,
by Patek Philippe, No. 863969, *circa* 1945, diameter 1⅜in (3.6cm)
New York $44,000 (£29,333). 16.VI.86
A gold chronograph wristwatch with tachometer, telemeter and registers, by Rolex, *circa* 1945,
diameter 1⅜in (3.6cm)
New York $14,300 (£9,533). 16.VI.86

Bottom row, left to right
A gold and stainless steel chronograph wristwatch with tachometer and registers, by
Patek Philippe, *circa* 1940, No. 862041, diameter 1¼in (3.2cm)
New York $7,150 (£4,767). 16.VI.86
A gold chronograph calendar wristwatch with moon phases by Audemars Piguet, No. 45983,
circa 1945, diameter 1⅜in (3.6cm)
New York $15,400 (£10,769). 30.X.85
A gold skeletonised self-winding perpetual calendar wristwatch with moon phases by Audemars
Piguet, No. 031 B86361, diameter 1⅜in (3.6cm)
New York $15,400 (£10,267). 16.VI.86

Musical instruments

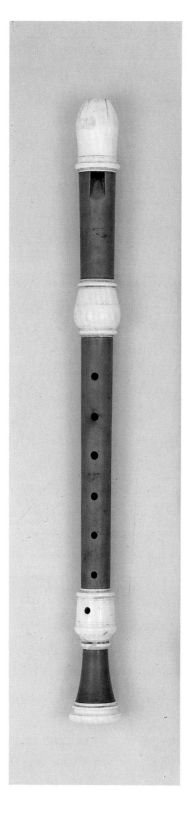

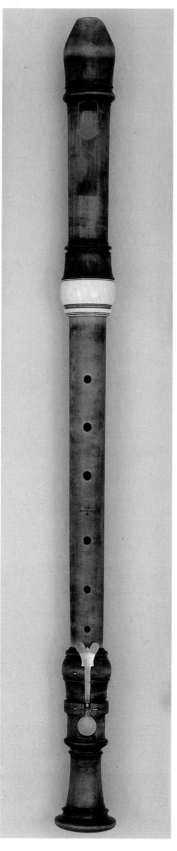

Left to right
A boxwood treble (alto) recorder by Rippert, Paris, last quarter seventeenth century, stamped *Rippert*, length 20½in (52.1cm)
London £12,100 ($18,029). 12.XII.85

A stained pearwood tenor recorder by Jean-Hyacinth-Joseph Rottenburgh, Brussels, first quarter eighteenth century, stamped *I.H. Rottenburgh*, length 26¾in (67.9cm)
London £14,300 ($21,307). 12.XII.85

A two-manual harpsichord by Andreas Ruckers, Antwerp, *circa* 1628, inscribed *Joannes Ruckers fecit Antverpiae 1628*, length 7ft 7½in (232.4cm)
London £68,200 ($101,618). 12.XII.85

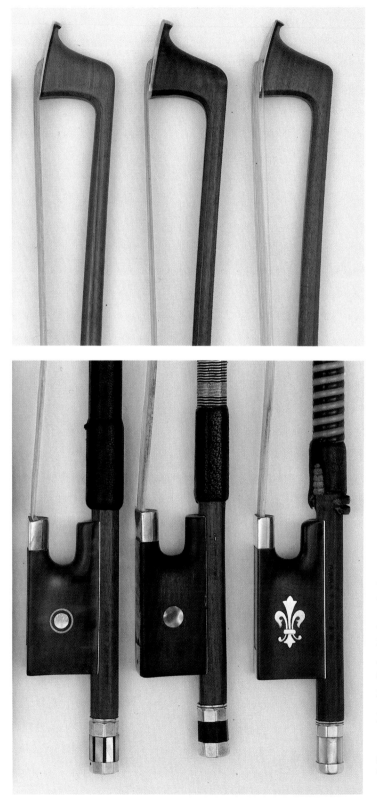

Left to right
A gold and tortoiseshell-mounted violin bow by Eugène Sartory, Paris, stamped *E. Sartory a Paris*, weight 59 grams
£4,840 ($7,163)

A French silver-mounted violin bow by Pajeot, stamped *Pajeot*, weight 57 grams
£3,520 ($5,210)

A gold and tortoiseshell-mounted violin bow by W.E. Hill & Sons, London, stamped *W.E.Hill & Sons*, weight 60 grams
£2,640 ($3,907)

These bows were sold in London on 14 November 1985.

The 'Ex-Carrodus' violin by Joseph Guarneri del Gesù, Cremona, *circa* 1741, labelled *Joseph Guarnerius Fecit Cremone Anno 1741 IHS*, length of back $13\frac{15}{16}$ in (35.4cm) London £214,500 ($328,185). 19.III.86
From the collection of the late Raymonde I. Paul

The 'Piatti' violin by Antonio Stradivari, Cremona, 1717, labelled *Antonius Stradivarius Cremonensis Faciebat Anno 1717 AS*, length of back $13\frac{15}{16}$ in (35.4cm) London £170,500 ($260,865). 19.III.86
From the collection of the late Raymonde I. Paul

Furniture and tapestries

A pair of George II carved walnut library armchairs, mid eighteenth century
New York $56,100 (£40,360). 25.I.86
From the collection of Jerome C. Neuhoff

A George II walnut games table, second quarter eighteenth century, width 3ft (91cm)
New York $49,500 (£35,612). 25.I.86

A George III gilt-wood sofa, *circa* 1760, length 10ft 5$\frac{7}{8}$in (319cm)
London £15,950 ($24,723). 28.II.86

Opposite
A George III painted and parcel-gilt armchair from a suite comprising a sofa and two armchairs,
circa 1780
London £18,700 ($29,920). 25.IV.86

A George III carved and inlaid mahogany breakfront bookcase, last quarter eighteenth century,
height 8ft 10in (269cm)
New York $99,000 (£71,223). 25.I.86
From the collection of Jerome C. Neuhoff

One of a pair of Regency mahogany *bergères, circa* 1810
London £23,100 ($35,805). 28.II.86

A George III satinwood-veneered writing table made for the Prince of Wales' use at Carlton House, *circa* 1785, width 5ft 1½in (156cm)
London £132,000 ($211,200). 25.IV.86

A serpentine front walnut writing desk, Ferrara, mid eighteenth century, width 7ft ¾in (215cm)
Florence L135,600,000 (£51,613:$74,323). 25.IX.85

A pair of Louis XVI ebony-veneered cabinets, set with bronze plaques and *pietra dura* and boulle
panels, attributed to Adam Weisweiler, height 3ft (91.5cm)
Monte Carlo FF4,551,000 (£423,349:$636,503). 22.VI.86
From the collection of the late Charles De Pauw

A Florentine *pietra dura* table top from the Grand Ducal workshops, *circa* 1680, 4ft 10¼in by 4ft 1¼in
(148cm by 125cm)
London £110,000 ($169,400). 29.XI.85

A Louis XV gilt-bronze-mounted lacquer commode attributed to Bernard van Risamburgh, width 5ft 2¼in (158cm)
New York $1,056,000 (£694,737). 3.V.86

A Louis XIV gilt-bronze-mounted console attributed to the workshops of André-Charles
Boulle, *circa* 1720, width 4ft 4⅜in (133cm)
Monte Carlo FF3,108,000 (£289,116: $434,685). 22.VI.86
From the collection of A. Roussel

One of a set of three Louis XVI gilt-bronze-mounted mahogany cabinets, signed
A. Weisweiler, last quarter eighteenth century, height 3ft 1¼in (94.6cm)
New York $264,000 (£185,915). 3.XI.85
From the collection of the late Sarah Jane Pansa

A Louis XVI gilt-bronze-mounted ebony-veneered commode with lacquer panels, stamped
A. Weisweiler, width 5ft 5¾in (167cm)
Monte Carlo FF6,105,000 (£567,910:$853,846). 22.VI.86
From the collection of the late Charles De Pauw

A pair of Louis XIV gilt-bronze candlesticks, early eighteenth century, height 1ft 3¾in (40cm)
London £46,200 ($72,996). 20.VI.86

Two of a set of four Louis XV/XVI gilt-bronze *bras de lumière*, third quarter eighteenth century, height 2ft (61cm)
New York $68,750 (£48,759). 12.X.85
From the collection of the Robert R. Young Foundation from the estate of Anita O'Keeffe Young

One of a pair of Louis XV bronze and gilt-bronze *chenets* in the form of a Triton, attributed to
Antoine Moureau, mid eighteenth century, height 1ft 4½in (42cm)
London £27,500 ($42,350). 29.XI.85

A Louis XVI gilt-wood *pliant*, bearing a stencilled label with the mark *S.C.* surmounted by a closed crown and the inscription *N° 11/12*, 1788, width 2ft 1in (63.5cm)
New York $85,250 (£60,035). 9.XI.85
From the collection of Nelson A. Rockefeller

This stool is one of a set of twelve made for the king's bedchamber at the château of Saint-Cloud by various craftsmen including Sené, Régnier, Vallois and Chatard.

A Brazilian rosewood side table inlaid with ivory, circle of Pietro Piffetti, Torino, *circa* 1740, width 4ft ¾in (124cm)
Florence L99,440,000 (£37,849:$54,503). 25.IX.85

Opposite
A Qianlong carved ivory slant dressing bureau, last quarter eighteenth century, height 5ft 11½in (181cm)
New York $82,500 (£57,292). 2.XI.85

The meeting of Jacob and Rachel by the well, one of a pair of Flemish or Sheldon cushion covers, *circa* 1600, 18in by 18in (46cm by 46cm)
Littlecote House £13,200 ($19,668). 20.XI.85

A William III armorial tapestry portière, from a design attributed to Daniel Marot, Brussels, *circa* 1690, 9ft by 7ft 9in (275cm by 237cm)
Littlecote House £33,000 ($49,830). 21.XI.85

Silver

A Gothic parcel-gilt ewer, maker's mark *A.I.*, probably Aragonese, late fifteenth–early
sixteenth century, height 8⅛in (20.5cm)
Geneva SF 264,000 (£94,712:$145,856). 13.V.86

Opposite
A German parcel-gilt Gothic beaker and cover, *circa* 1425, height 14⅜in (36.5cm)
Geneva SF 792,000 (£284,136:$437,569). 13.V.86

An inscription on the inside identifies this covered beaker as the property of the
illustrious von Glauburg family.

A gold beaker and cover with twenty-eight enamelled bosses bearing the arms and names of Thuringian families, probably Dresden, *circa* 1750, height 9⅛in (23.3cm) Geneva SF 440,000 (£136,646:$202,236) 12.XI.85

The finial is a princely crown, probably relating to the elevation in 1710 of the House of Schwarzburg to the Imperial College, although Count Ludwig Friedrich I did not take his seat in the Reichstag until 1754, when this beaker was probably presented to him by the local nobility.

Opposite
A parcel-gilt nef, maker's mark of Esaias zur Linden, Nuremberg, *circa* 1620, height 22in (55.8cm) Geneva SF 473,000 (£169,692:$261,326). 13.V.86

A Louis XVI silver-gilt ewer and basin, engraved with the crests of William Beckford, designed by Jean-Guillaume Moitte, maker's mark of Henry Auguste, Paris, 1789, diameter of basin 13¾in (35cm); height of ewer 17¼in (43.8cm)
New York $154,000 (£106,207). 8.IV.86

Twelve designs for goldsmiths, chiefly for Henry Auguste, by Jean-Guillaume Moitte, were sold at Sotheby's in Monte Carlo on 22 February 1986, including one for a pair of basins which belonged to William Beckford. The basin illustrated is one of these, the other was sold at Sotheby's in Monte Carlo on 24 June 1986. Both were sold with their ewers.

A George III silver-gilt tea urn, makers' mark of Digby Scott and Benjamin Smith, for
Rundell, Bridge & Rundell, London, 1805, height 15in (38.1cm)
New York $99,000 (£68,276). 8.IV.86

A pair of Charles I wine cups bearing the arms of Barnard's Inn and inscribed, maker's mark a
bow and arrow between *WS* for Walter Shute, London, 1627, height 10⅝in (27cm)
London £96,800 ($152,944). 19.VI.86

A set of twenty-four Queen Anne dinner plates, bearing the arms of Monckton impaling Manners, maker's mark of Philip Rollos, London, 1706, diameter 9½in (24.2cm)
New York $187,000 (£132,624). 10.X.85
From the collection of the Robert R. Young Foundation from the estate of Anita O'Keeffe Young

A Charles II 'wager-cup' automaton, maker's mark *RB* with a mullet below in a shaped shield, *circa* 1680, height 7in (17.9cm)
London £50,600 ($75,900). 24.X.85

A pair of George II candlesticks, maker's mark of Paul de Lamerie, London, 1742, height 11in (28cm)
London £275,000 ($434,500). 19.VI.86

A set of four George IV silver-gilt candlesticks, maker's mark of John Bridge, for Rundell, Bridge
& Rundell, London, 1828, height 12¼in (31cm)
London £31,900 ($47,850). 24.X.85

A Victorian silver-gilt racing trophy, inscribed on the reverse, maker's mark of John Samuel Hunt,
for Hunt & Roskell, London, 1843, diameter 29in (73.7cm)
London £52,800 ($77,088). 6.II.86

The inscription on the reverse reads *Won by Emperor*.

European ceramics
and glass

A Chelsea polychrome figure of Hogarth's dog Trump, after a lost original by Roubiliac,
1745–47, length 11in (28cm)
London £85,800 ($137,280). 1.VII.86
From the Rous Lench Collection

A Whieldon model of a dovecote, *circa* 1755, height 7¾in (19.7cm)
London £30,800 ($46,200). 25.II.86
From the collection of the late Captain C.B. Kidd

A saltglaze pew group, *circa* 1745, height 6½in (16.6cm)
London £112,200 ($179,520). 1.VII.86
From the Rous Lench Collection

A saltglaze bell figure of a lady in a crinoline dress, *circa* 1740, height 4⅜in (11cm)
London £52,800 ($84,480). 1.VII.86
From the Rous Lench Collection

A portrait charger of Charles II, signed with monogram *NT* and dated *1666*, diameter 13in (33cm)
London £85,800 ($137,280). 1.VII.86
From the Rous Lench Collection

Opposite
A Staffordshire slipware jug, signed *DS* and dated *1704*, height 9in (23cm)
London £55,000 ($88,000). 1.VII.86
From the Rous Lench Collection

A Barr, Flight and Barr tea service, *circa* 1807
London £19,800 ($31,086). 27.V.86

Opposite, centre
A Chelsea 'Hans Sloane' plate, *circa* 1758, diameter 9⅛in (23.2cm), $10,450 (£7,411)
Opposite, clockwise from top left
A Chelsea 'Hans Sloane' plate, red anchor mark, *circa* 1758, diameter 9⅛in (23.2cm), $6,050 (£4,291)
A Chelsea 'Hans Sloane' plate, red anchor mark, *circa* 1758, diameter 9¼in (23.5cm), $11,000 (£7,801)
A Chelsea 'Hans Sloane' plate, *circa* 1758, diameter 9⅛in (23.2cm), $7,700 (£5,461)
A Chelsea 'Hans Sloane' plate, *circa* 1758, diameter 9⅛in (23.2cm), $7,700 (£5,461)
A Chelsea 'Hans Sloane' plate, red anchor mark, *circa* 1758, diameter 9⅛in (23.2cm), $7,700 (£5,461)
A Chelsea 'Hans Sloane' plate, *circa* 1758, diameter 9¼in (23.5cm), $4,950 (£3,511)
A Chelsea 'Hans Sloane' plate, black anchor mark, *circa* 1758, diameter 9⅛in (23.2cm), $5,500 (£3,901)
A Chelsea 'Hans Sloane' plate, red anchor mark, *circa* 1758, diameter 9⅛in (23.2cm), $9,350 (£6,631)

The plates illustrated on the opposite page are from the collection of the Robert R. Young Foundation from the estate of Anita O'Keeffe Young and were sold in New York on 10 October 1985.

A Faenza maiolica portrait vase, *circa* 1480, height 12¼in (31cm)
London £22,000 ($34,760). 17.VI.86

A Nymphenburg figure of an egg-seller, modelled by Franz Anton Bustelli, impressed
shield mark and *i*, *circa* 1755, height 5⅝in (14.5cm)
London £27,500 ($41,250). 4.III.86

An Ellwangen snuff box, painted by Johann A. Bechdolff, *circa* 1758, width 3in (7.6cm)
London £25,300 ($39,974). 17.VI.86

One of a pair of Louis XV gilt-bronze-mounted Meissen covered potpourri jars, crowned *C* mark, the guinea fowl modelled by Johann Joachim Kaendler, 1742–49, height 11¾in (29.9cm)
New York $96,250 (£68,262). 10.X.85
From the collection of the Robert R. Young Foundation from the estate of Anita O'Keeffe Young

A Meissen chinoiserie yellow-ground garniture, the large vase marked *AR*, the pair marked with crossed swords in underglaze blue, *circa* 1740, heights 18⅝in (47.4cm) and 19⅞in (50.5cm) respectively
New York $121,000 (£85,211). 8.XI.85
From the collection of Nelson A. Rockefeller

A Meissen 'Augustus Rex' vase and cover, *circa* 1730, marked *AR* in blue, height 10¾in (27.2cm)
London £17,600 ($26,928). 26.XI.85

A transparent-enamelled topographical beaker decorated
by Samuel Mohn, signed, Dresden, *circa* 1810,
height 4⅛in (10.3cm)
London £16,500 ($24,255). 10.II.86

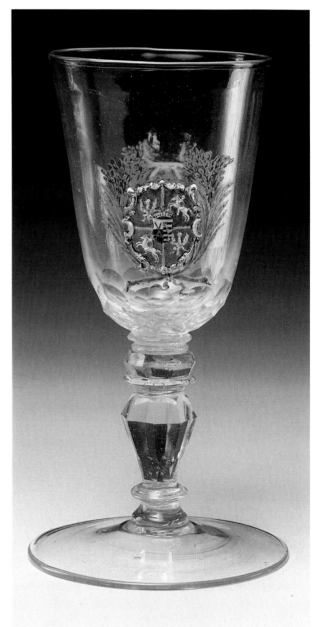

A Saxon relief-enamelled royal armorial goblet, decorated
by Johann Heinrich Meyer, Dresden, *circa* 1730,
height 7¼in (18.5cm)
London £11,000 ($16,170). 10.II.86

On one side the goblet is decorated with the arms of
Saxony in relief in colours, while the reverse bears the
monogram *AR*, for Augustus the Strong, in relief and
highlighted in garnets.

Left
A Baccarat thousand petalled rose weight,
diameter 3⅛in (8cm)
New York $5,775 (£3,955). 12.III.86

Right
A Baccarat flat bouquet weight,
diameter 3⅛in (8cm)
New York $10,725 (£7,346). 12.III.86
From the collection of the Bergstrom
Art Center

Right
A Baccarat gentian weight,
diameter 2⅞in (7.4cm)
New York $8,800 (£6,027)
12.III.86

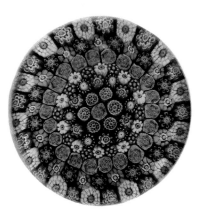

Left
A Clichy concentric millefiori piedouche
weight, diameter 2¾in (7cm)
New York $9,075 (£6,216). 12.III.86

Right
A Pantin bouquet weight,
diameter 3¼in (8.3cm)
New York $7,150 (£4,897). 12.III.86

The work of Ammi Phillips and his contemporaries: paintings from the Tillou Collection

Mary Black

Ammi Phillips' career as an itinerant painter is briefly outlined in three paintings from Peter Tillou's collection of American folk painting sold at Sotheby's, New York, in late October 1985. A number of other portraits in the collection by contemporaries and earlier artists in territories that coincided or overlapped Phillips' own, hint at influences that may have affected his style. These images of long-vanished patrons recapture an era in which an informal guild of travelling limners plied their trade.

Phillips was born in Colebrook, Connecticut in the spring of 1788. Within a limited territory that extended as far west and south as Putnam, Orange, Schoharie and Schenectady Counties in New York, and east to the banks of the Connecticut in New England, Phillips spent fifty amazingly productive years. By 1812 he had already begun his journeying and had painted several portraits of Berkshire County, Massachusetts subjects. The six that survive are of adults and children in three prosperous households in Stockbridge, Great Barrington, and Sheffield. In the dozen years that followed, Phillips travelled in western New England and eastern New York, regions that gave him identity as the 'Border Limner'.

In the painter's 'Border period', from about 1813 to 1820, the dark backgrounds of his earliest work were supplanted by light warm greys, in a palette so pale and refined that it seems possible that he might have initially worked as a pastellist. While the source of this changed palette is unknown, it seems clear that an evolution and development in his method, from the two-dimensional subjects of his earliest work where the heads seem flattened, came from a knowledge of other painters' style. His use of lightened colour is seen in the earliest of his portraits in the Tillou sale, an unidentified *Man holding a quill, circa* 1813. One possible inspiration for the improved shape of the head in this waist-length painting might have been his familiarity with likenesses by J. Brown, a mysterious figure who earlier worked in his territory between 1803 and 1808. Yet no one would confuse Brown's work with Phillips', and the over large hands, wispy hair, lined upper eyelids and awkward anatomy of *Man holding a quill* are seen again in *Ruth Haynes*

Fig. 1
Attributed to Ammi Phillips
A YOUNG GIRL IN A WHITE DRESS: MISS RUTH HAYNES (PALMER) OF HOOSICK, NEW YORK
Circa 1818, 36in by 30in (91.5cm by 76.2cm)
New York $181,500 (£127,817). 26.X.85
From the collection of Peter Tillou

Fig. 2
Attributed to Erastus Salisbury Field
GIRL ON A STENCILLED CARPET
34in by 26in (86.3cm by 66cm)
New York $66,000 (£46,479). 26.X.85

The paintings illustrated on these pages are from the collection of Peter Tillou.

Fig. 3
Attributed to Joseph Whiting Stock
JANE TYLER
Circa 1845, 39¾in by 30in (101cm by 76.2cm)
New York $77,000 (£54,225). 26.X.85

Palmer, a subject painted by Phillips, *circa* 1818 (Fig. 1). The artist was then in Hoosick, New York where he painted likenesses of Ruth's parents, John and Phebe Peck Haynes, and of other residents.

In his portrait of this young woman Phillips reverted to the dark backgrounds of his earliest work, a practice that he continued in most of the likenesses from the 1820s onwards. A change in the positioning of his subjects in the 1830s earned Phillips, in the early years of this century, the title of the 'Kent Limner', for works he produced in and around Kent, Connecticut and in neighbouring New York counties. The women of the 1830s are posed leaning gracefully forward, and they, along with the full-length portraits of children of this decade, are among the works most prized by collectors.

Phillips' path frequently crossed those of other itinerant painters, most notably that of an artist who was almost as prolific as he was, Erastus Salisbury Field (1805–1900), who was born in Leverett, Massachusetts. The pose of a little girl on a stencilled carpet seen in Field's full-length portrait in the Tillou sale (Fig. 2) suggests that he might have seen and adapted a Phillips composition to his own use. A further stylistic echo is sounded in another portrait from the collection by Joseph Whiting Stock of a little girl, *Jane Tyler* (Fig. 3), dressed in pink and standing on a figured carpet. Stock (1815–55), a crippled artist born in Springfield, Massachusetts, travelled the same New England circuit as his contemporaries, Phillips and Field.

In 1823 and 1824 and again in the early 1830s Phillips went farthest from his home territory to work in Orange and Greene Counties, New York. A decade after he left this area west of the Hudson, Stock appeared there to spend the last years of his life serving families who had formerly called on Phillips for a record of faces, figures and environments.

In the 1840s Phillips lived and worked in and around Amenia, New York, but by the 1850s he had returned to the Berkshires, buying a house in Curtisville (now Interlaken), Massachusetts where he worked for the rest of his life. The camera had by then come into common use, depriving face painters of a vocation that had once been a valuable service to patrons, and one that had given its practitioners a profitable livelihood. Phillips was almost the last among his contemporaries to paint from life, clinging to this method long after photographs began to be used for the poses, faces and backgrounds seen in the late work of both Field and Stock. In some late portraits of the late 1850s or early 1860s Phillips used photographs as a guide, but the *Family portrait* of a boy and his grandmother (Fig. 4) shows that he continued to borrow elements from his own earlier work for compositions and details that remained remarkably consistent throughout a long career.

Almost twenty years ago a Phillips biography set forth this artist as the near-perfect example of a self-taught painter. At that time some three hundred of his portraits were known. Today more than five hundred examples have been identified and illustrate why this prolific artist's portraits are the most sought after of any of the self-taught fraternity.

Fig. 4
Attributed to Ammi Phillips
FAMILY PORTRAIT
1850–60, 36in by 38in (91.5cm by 96.5cm)
New York $110,000 (£77,465). 26.X.85
From the collection of Peter Tillou

American decorative arts and furniture

Charles C. Hofmann
VIEW OF THE SCHUYLKILL COUNTY ALMSHOUSE PROPERTY, PA
Signed with the artist's initials, inscribed and dated *1875*, and inscribed *Positively no Admittance on Sunday/Visitors to the almshouse will/be admitted only on Thursday/of each week from 9 a.m. to /5 p.m.*,
31in by 43in (78.7cm by 109.2cm)
New York $126,500 (£89,716). 1.II.86

A needlework sampler, probably Newburyport, Massachusetts, late eighteenth-early nineteenth century, 16¼in by 17½in (41.2cm by 44.5cm)
New York $101,750 (£72,163). 1.II.86

A silver salver bearing the Barrett arms, maker's mark of John Coburn, Boston, *circa* 1760,
diameter 13in (33cm)
New York $85,250 (£56,457). 26.VI.86
From the collection of the late Francis A. Wendell

A silver tankard, maker's mark of Henricus Boelen II, New York, *circa* 1720,
height 7¼in (18.5cm)
New York $51,700 (£36,667). 31.I.86
From the collection of the Robert R. Young Foundation from the estate of
Anita O'Keeffe Young

A pair of Queen Anne carved walnut side chairs, Rhode Island, *circa* 1755
New York $110,000 (£72,848). 26.VI.86

A Queen Anne figured maple lowboy, Stonington Area, Connecticut, *circa* 1765,
width 2ft 7¾in (80.7cm)
New York $170,500 (£112,914). 26.VI.86
From the collection of the late Evelyn Kleven Gottlieb Zamboni

A Chippendale carved mahogany chest of drawers, Massachusetts, *circa* 1770, width 36½in (92.7cm)
New York $159,500 (£112,324). 26.X.85

Opposite
A Chippendale carved mahogany longcase clock, the case labelled *James McDowell*, Delaware,
the painted dial possibly by Beard and Weaver, Delaware, *circa* 1785, height 8ft ½in (244cm)
New York $66,000 (£46,809). 1.II.86
From the collection of the late Mr and Mrs John N. Berger

A Chippendale carved mahogany marble top pier table, attributed to John Goddard, Newport,
Rhode Island, *circa* 1765, width 4ft 3¼in (130cm)
New York $330,000 (£218,543). 26.VI.86

A pair of Chippendale carved mahogany armchairs, attributed to the Townsend family, Newport,
Rhode Island, *circa* 1765
New York $154,000 (£109,220). 1.II.86

The Cornelius C. Moore Collection of early American silver

American silver of the late seventeenth and early eighteenth century is extremely rare. Only about one in twenty of the early settlers owned silver, and many colonists persisted in buying British and Continental wares until well into the eighteenth century. For the most part, the early silversmiths produced table silver, cups and tankards, porringers and teapots, pepper-boxes (see opposite), ladles and spoons, and all these forms were well-represented in the Cornelius C. Moore collection.

Mr Moore, a lawyer and a banker, was a lifelong resident of Newport, Rhode Island. Known today as a fashionable summer resort, Newport was first settled in 1639 and rapidly became one of the most prosperous colonies. The economic stability and religious tolerance that prevailed there fostered the development of the arts, distinguished by an exceptionally high level of craftsmanship. Mr Moore was well known as a collector of American furniture and paintings as well as silver, concentrating primarily on Newport works.

His silver collection presents an interesting survey of eighteenth-century work, with virtually every significant New York, Boston, Philadelphia, and Newport maker represented. Among the finest examples were a porringer by Thomas Arnold, the first silversmith known in the state, and a group of fourteen pieces by Samuel Casey, including a particularly handsome teapot (see opposite). A substantial group of Boston silver included pieces by three generations of the Edwards family, John, his sons Thomas and Samuel, and a grandson, Joseph, Jr, that span a seventy-year period, and a selection of small but elegant pieces, spoons, a pair of sugar tongs and a creamer by Paul Revere, the Patriot.

The development of a more elaborate style in the mid-eighteenth century is seen in the work of the New York and Philadelphia silversmiths, particularly Myer Myers and Joseph Richardson, Sr. A covered sugar bowl by Myers was noteworthy both for its handsome proportions and for its history of use as an etrog container in the Touro Synagogue in Newport. Designed by Peter Harrison and dedicated in 1763, Touro is the oldest synagogue in the United States. The Richardson salver is a wonderful example of Philadelphia rococo, with a swirling shell and ribbon border and an elaborate engraved cypher for Francis and Rebecca Rawle.

Mr Moore bequeathed his silver collection to Providence College, one of a number of Rhode Island institutions that he supported, and the college was the beneficiary of the auction, which totalled more than $600,000.

A teapot, maker's mark of Samuel Casey, Exeter and South Kingston, Rhode Island, *circa* 1765,
height 6⅞in (17.5cm)
New York $30,800 (£21,844)

Left to right
An octagonal pepper-box, maker's mark of Andrew Oliver, Boston,
circa 1740, height 4⅜in (11.2cm) $7,150 (£5,071)
An octagonal pepper-box, maker's mark of Jacob Hurd, Boston,
circa 1730–40, height 3⅝in (9.2cm) $7,150 (£5,071)

The silver illustrated on this page is from the collection of the late
Cornelius C. Moore and was sold in New York on 31 January 1986.

Nineteenth-century
decorative arts

A polychrome boulle centre table by Franz Xavier Fortner, Munich, signed and dated *1843*,
width 3ft 7¼in (110.5cm)
London £49,500 ($74,250). 8.XI.85

A pair of lapis lazuli and gilt-bronze columns, mid nineteenth century, height 7ft 5in (226cm)
London £88,000 ($140,800). 13.VI.86

A Coalbrookdale cast-iron centre table supported by four life-size parcel-gilt deerhounds, designed by John Bell, length 6ft 2in (188cm)
London £63,800 ($95,700). 8.XI.85
From the collection of Mrs Diana Quentin Wallace

This table was made for the 1855 *Exposition Universelle* in Paris.

A Berlin plaque, painted by Maltz, signed, impressed mark, *circa* 1880, 10⅝in by 22½in (27cm by 56.5cm)
London £13,200 ($19,800). 7.XI.85

A gilt-bronze-mounted marble urn clock, signed *Millet a Paris*, the bell striking A.D. Mougin movement No. 427, signed *Maline Horloger*, third quarter nineteenth century, height 28½in (72.5cm)
London £18,150 ($28,314). 21.III.86

A white marble and bronze bust of an Arab man by Pietro Calvi, signed, *circa* 1880,
height 35½in (90cm)
London £16,500 ($26,400). 12.VI.86

Opposite
The Bartholdi family bronze figure of *Liberty Enlightening the World*, by Frédéric-Auguste Bartholdi,
inscribed *A. Bartholdi* and *Thiebaut Fres*, *circa* 1885, height 53½in (136cm)
New York $148,500 (£99,664). 30.XI.85

This bronze reduction of the famous monumental statue in New York harbour was cast by
Thiebaut Frères for Bartholdi and had remained in the sculptor's family until the November sale.
Only a few other small bronzes were cast, and these are believed to have been made as presentation
pieces to those who worked to raise funds for the construction of the statue's pedestal.

A gilt-bronze and lapis lazuli boudoir timepiece, Paris, *circa* 1900, height 10in (25.4cm)
London £11,550 ($18,018). 21.III.86
A pair of gilt-bronze and Minton porcelain candelabra, *circa* 1845, height 10¾in (27.5cm)
London £3,300 ($5,148). 21.III.86

A silver, hardstone and ivory group of a young fisherman and a companion, German, late
nineteenth century, height 15⅛in (38.5cm)
London £25,300 ($39,721). 20.III.86

Opposite
A pair of Sèvres gilt-bronze-mounted *jardinières*, Paris, mid nineteenth century, height 16⅛in (41cm)
London £9,020 ($14,161). 20.III.86

Art Nouveau and Art Deco

A patinated and lacquered metal vase designed by Jean Dunand, signed and numbered *5129*,
circa 1925, height 5⅞in (15cm)
Monte Carlo FF721,500 (£65,591:$98,163). 13.IV.86

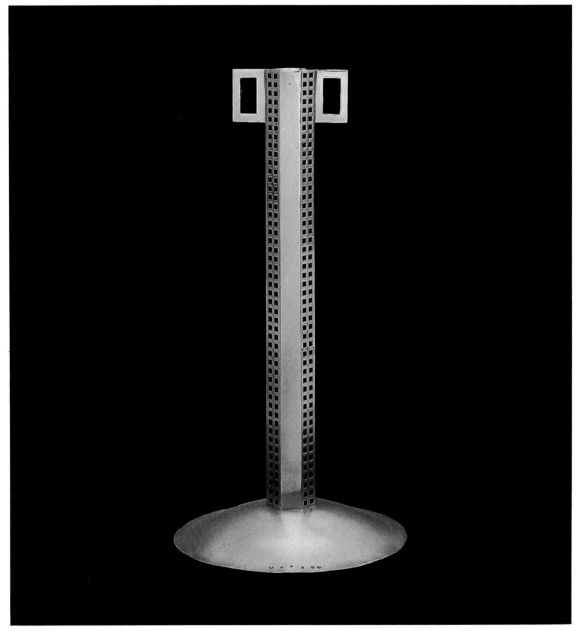

A Wiener Werkstätte silver vase designed by Josef Hoffmann, signed with monogram, *circa* 1904, height 14in (35.5cm)
Monte Carlo FF244,200 (£22,200:$33,224). 13.IV.86

An Aesthetic Movement stained and painted glass screen, *circa* 1880, height 6ft 8¼in (204cm)
London £28,600 ($45,474). 16.V.86

A double door with leaded glass panels designed by Frank Lloyd Wright, *circa* 1913, height of panels 5ft ⅛in (153cm) Monte Carlo FF199,800 (£17,374:$24,975). 6.X.85

A pair of shagreen and inlaid ivory commodes, designed by Paul Poiret for Atelier Martine and made by Adolphe Chanaux, *circa* 1921, height 27in (68.6cm)
New York $66,000 (£44,595). 7.XII.85

Two ivory and silver candelabra, with figures carved by Égide Rombaux, and silver
by Franz Hoosemans, *circa* 1900, height 14½in (36.9cm)
New York $45,100 (£30,268). 20.VI.86

A Loetz iridescent glass and hammered copper panel
designed by Georg Klimt, *circa* 1900, height 4ft 2in (127cm)
New York $57,750 (£39,020). 7.XII.85

Opposite
A silvered-bronze and black Belgian marble console and
mirror, designed by Albert Cheuret, *circa* 1920,
height 6ft 1¾in (187.6cm)
New York $86,900 (£58,322). 20.VI.86

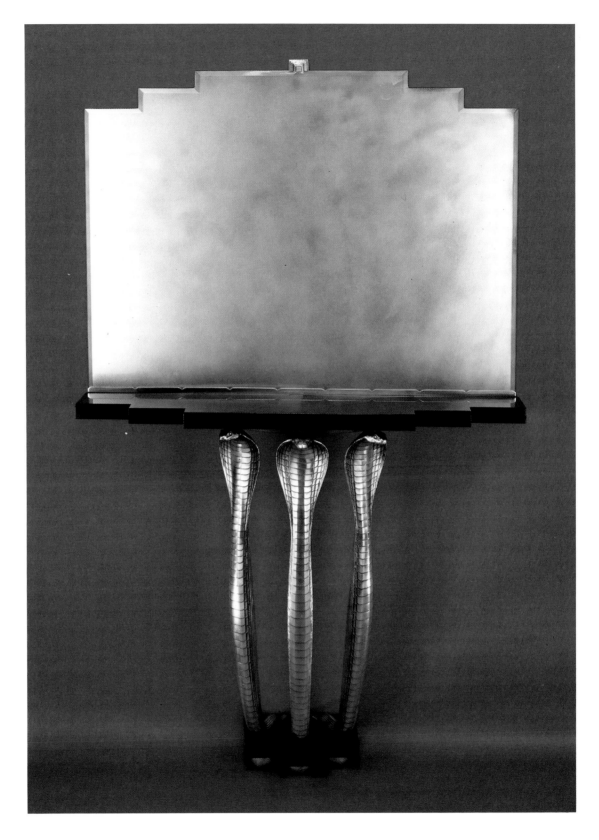

John Sheldon of Bentley & Co., Bond Street

John Culme

Electrifying both trade and private buyers alike, the disposal of the late John Sheldon's collection of jewellery and silver was a remarkable event. Mr Sheldon, well known as the proprietor of Bentley & Co., and doyen of the Bond Street retail jewellers, had managed in a long career to remain a private, even a remote figure at the same time earning respect among his fellow traders as a shrewd businessman, and with his customers for the consistently high quality of his stock.

John Sheldon was born Jean Schlounde, otherwise Schlund, at Mulhausen in 1902, the son of Léon Schlounde and Juliet Lipman of Cracow. After an eventful early career working in gold fields as far apart as Siberia and South Africa, Léon was forced to moderate his activities by the onslaught of arthritis. He moved with his family in 1904 or 1905 to London where he commenced trading as Léon Schlund & Co., or the London Refining & Metallurgical Works.

It soon became necessary for Jean, aged fourteen, to leave school to join his father. Afterwards regretting this move, the boy nevertheless was able to develop a grasp of business matters and, with his father's retirement in 1926, John Sheldon took control of the firm. He then began to indulge his own interests by trading as a wholesale jeweller as well as a bullion dealer, setting aside some of the made-up items he had purchased for breaking but which he realised were too good to scrap. These pieces became the nucleus of Mr Sheldon's collection which, upon the outbreak of war in 1939, were stored away until after his death on 6 February 1985.

By the mid-1930s, when the refining work of his firm was declining, John Sheldon's interest in jewellery dictated a change in direction. Almost with reluctance he purchased in 1934 for £500 the small West End jewellers, Bentley & Co., on the first floor at 65, New Bond Street. Six years later, when the shop below became vacant, he took the entire building where Bentley's has been ever since.

Bentley & Co.'s subsequent reputation was built upon John Sheldon's hard work. With the appearance at Sotheby's of his own collection, including some of the most important privately owned groups of antique and Giuliano jewellery ever to have been sold at auction, we saw for the first time his personal selection of pieces. It was appropriate that some of the items Mr Sheldon loved best, those from the workshops of Carl Fabergé for instance, were reminders of his family's native land.

Centre
A gold, enamel and jewelled necklace by Carlo and Arthur Giuliano, *circa* 1890,
£34,100 ($50,809)
A gold, enamel and jewelled pendant by Carlo Giuliano, *circa* 1870, £14,300 ($21,307)

The jewellery illustrated on this page is from the collection of the late John Sheldon and
was sold in London on 29 October 1985.

Jewellery

A diamond tiara, probably by Boucheron, *circa* 1910
London £23,100 ($34,188). 3.X.85

Clockwise from top left
A diamond brooch, last quarter nineteenth century, £6,600 ($9,834)
A diamond brooch, last quarter nineteenth century, £9,350 ($13,932)
A gold, turquoise, carbuncle and diamond necklace, *circa* 1840, £3,850 ($5,737)
A diamond brooch-pendant, eighteenth century, £2,750 ($4,098)
A diamond brooch, *circa* 1830, £2,640 ($3,934)
A diamond brooch, last quarter nineteenth century, £4,620 ($6,884)

The jewellery illustrated on this page is from the collection of the late John Sheldon and was sold in London on 29 October 1985.

A platinum and diamond necklace by Van Cleef & Arpels, $74,250 (£48,849)
A platinum and diamond double-clip brooch by Van Cleef & Arpels, $28,600 (£18,816)

The jewellery illustrated on this page was sold in New York on 10 June 1986.

A platinum and diamond pendent necklace, *circa* 1910, $8,525 (£6,046)
A gold, silver and diamond flower brooch, mid nineteenth century, $12,100 (£8,582)
A pair of platinum and diamond pendent earrings, *circa* 1910, $13,200 (£9,362)
A pair of diamond swallow earrings, $15,400 (£10,922)

The jewellery illustrated on this page was sold in New York on 15 October 1985.

The Isabel Anderson emerald, mid nineteenth century
New York $297,000 (£198,000). 16.IV.86

Isabel Anderson, a distinguished writer of travel
books, describes in *Odd Corners* her presentation at
court in London in 1904, wearing 'on my corsage a
big Indian emerald which a maharaja had worn in
the front of his turban'.

An Edwardian emerald and diamond brooch, *circa* 1910
Geneva SF99,000 (£30,745:$45,503). 13.XI.85

Opposite
A triple-strand pearl necklace by Van Cleef & Arpels
Geneva SF935,000 (£337,630:$516,575). 14.V.86

An emerald and diamond necklace and a pair of pendent earrings, *circa* 1880
Geneva SF836,000 (£259,627:$384,248). 13.XI.85

A gold, platinum, peridot and diamond fantasy necklace by Charles Vaillant, designed by
Salvador Dali, *circa* 1965, $132,000 (£86,842)
A gold, peridot and diamond ring by Charles Vaillant, $8,250 (£5,428)

The jewellery illustrated on this page was sold in New York on 10 June 1986.

A jade, onyx, lapis lazuli and diamond clock by Ostertag, *circa* 1910
St Moritz SF 132,000 (£45,051:$68,478). 21.II.86

Opposite
A pair of emerald, diamond and pearl pendent earrings, nineteenth century, $13,200 (£8,684)
From the collection of Ms Liv Faret
A seed pearl and diamond wristwatch by Cartier, *circa* 1915, $18,700 (£12,303)
A carved emerald and diamond wristwatch by Cartier, *circa* 1930, $27,500 (£18,092)
A platinum and diamond ring-watch by Cartier, *circa* 1935, $14,850 (£9,770)

The jewellery illustrated on the opposite page was sold in New York on 10 June 1986.

A diamond rivière by Cartier, SF682,000 (£244,672:$376,796)
A pair of diamond single-stone earrings by Cartier, SF253,000 (£90,766:$139,779)
A diamond bracelet by Cartier, SF385,000 (£138,122:$212,707)

A ruby and diamond necklace, first half nineteenth century
Geneva SF 308,000 (£110,497:$170,166)

The jewellery illustrated on these pages is from the collection of the late Countess Mona Bismarck
and was sold in Geneva on 13 May 1986.

A platinum and diamond necklace with detachable brooch by Harry Winston
New York $220,000 (£156,028). 16.X.85

A Burmese cultured pearl necklace
New York $550,000 (£390,071). 16.X.85

A triple-strand Burmese cultured pearl necklace
New York $286,000 (£190,667). 16.IV.86

Top left to bottom right
A sapphire and diamond ring SF33,000 (£11,916:$18,232)
A sapphire and diamond bracelet SF572,000 (£206,550:$316,022)
From the collection of the late Charles De Pauw
A sapphire and diamond ring SF121,000 (£43,693:$66,851)

The jewellery illustrated on this page was sold in Geneva on 14 May 1986.

A gold, black opal, sapphire, diamond and enamel pendent watch and chain by Marcus & Co.,
circa 1900, $28,600 (£19,067)
A black opal, enamel and diamond ring, *circa* 1900, $11,000 (£7,333)
A black opal and diamond pendant-brooch by Marcus & Co., *circa* 1900, $9,350 (£6,233)

The jewellery illustrated on this page is from the collection of the late Miss Claudia Lea Phelps and
was sold in New York on 16 April 1986.

A diamond, ruby and emerald ballerina brooch by Van Cleef & Arpels, *circa* 1940, $41,800 (£29,645)
A pair of diamond, ruby and emerald ballerina earrings by Van Cleef & Arpels, *circa* 1940, $17,600 (£12,482)

The ballerina jewellery illustrated above is from the collection of the late Mrs B. Joseph Hammond and was sold in New York on 10 December 1985.

A pair of diamond pendent earrings by Harry Winston
New York $137,500 (£97,518). 16.X.85

A platinum and diamond ring by Harry Winston
New York
$253,000 (£179,433)
10.XII.85
From the collection of the late Una Chapman Cox

A platinum and diamond ring by Harry Winston
New York
$357,500 (£238,333)
16.IV.86

A sapphire and diamond ring
New York
$220,000 (£146,667)
16.IV.86

A diamond ring
New York
$462,000 (£327,660)
16.X.85

Antiquities and Asian art

A translucent amethyst coloured mosaic glass bowl, Eastern Mediterranean,
late second–mid first century BC, diameter $5\frac{1}{4}$in (13.4cm)
London £57,200 ($87,516). 9.XII.85
From the collection of the Corning Museum of Glass, New York

A silver bowl, Central Asia, probably Bactria, first–fifth century AD, diameter 8¼in (21cm)
London £88,000 ($134,640). 9.XII.85
From the collection of Professor David Snellgrove

A red-figure stemless cup, Attic, *circa* 480 BC, diameter 5⅞in (15cm)
New York $45,100 (£30,680). 30.V.86
From the collection of the late Professor Jakob Rosenberg

Opposite
A marble head of Zeus Ammon, Alexandrian, first half second century AD, height 19in (48.2cm)
New York $132,000 (£92,308). 21.XI.85
From the collection of the Art League of Daytona Beach

A bronze statuette of a youthful warrior,
Greek, *circa* 530 BC, found in South Arabia,
height 6⅝in (17cm)
London £52,800 ($82,368). 14.VII.86
From the collection of Andrew Altounyan

A granite figure of Sekhmet enthroned, Thebes, Eighteenth Dynasty, reign of
Amenhotep III, 1403–1365 BC, height 82½in (209.5cm)
New York $742,500 (£505,102). 30.V.86
From the collection of the late John Lennon

A Chola bronze figure of Siva as Lord of Music, *circa* eleventh century, height 29½in (75cm) New York $154,000 (£115,789) 20.IX.85

Opposite
A Tibetan *Thang-ka* (scroll painting) depicting the Dharmapala Mahakala as Protector of the Tent, Ngor, *circa* seventeenth century, 20⅞in by 16⅞in (53cm by 43cm) London £18,700 ($30,294) 7.VII.86

A loan exhibition of classical antiquities in aid of the Ashmole Archive

Carlos A. Picón

In January 1986 a loan exhibition of classical art from private collections in Great Britain was held in the Kiddell Gallery at Sotheby's, New Bond Street. The exhibition was organised to launch an appeal in aid of the Ashmole Archive, now in the keeping of the Department of Classics at King's College, London. This unique archive consists of more than 10,000 photographs of Greek and Roman sculptures acquired during a lifetime's distinguished research by Professor Bernard Ashmole, formerly Director of the British School at Rome, Yates Professor of Classical Archaeology at London University, Keeper of Greek and Roman Antiquities at the British Museum, and Lincoln Professor of Classical Archaeology at Oxford University. The Ashmole Archive is already open to the public. The ongoing appeal, however, aims to raise sufficient funds not only to provide for a full-time curatorial staff, but also to expand the present collection into an international centre for the study of ancient sculpture. It is to be hoped that this year's successful and generous response both from those who loaned pieces and from British, European, as well as American benefactors will continue unabated.

The exhibition featured sixty-seven Greek and Roman antiquities, ranging from a Cycladic marble idol of *circa* 2500 BC to Roman portraits of the third century AD. Loans from the great country houses included an idealised head of an athlete from Petworth and another of Zeus from Holkham Hall, a Roman cinerary urn and a triangular pedestal from Broadlands, portrait busts from Chatsworth, Syon House, Woburn Abbey, Kingston Lacy, and from the collection of Lord Elgin at Broomhall in Fife. The outstanding collections at Harrow School, Eton College, Charterhouse and Winchester School were also represented by notable examples of Greek pottery, marble sculptures, bronzes and minor arts. Many of the objects, however, came from lesser-known sources and had never been on public view before. Other exhibits were chosen with an eye for the unusual, such as a colossal foot made of porphyry, once in the Hope Collection, and a large Roman marble ship restored in the eighteenth century, possibly by Piranesi.

One of the benefits of a loan exhibition comprising primarily unpublished material is the opportunity to study the objects at greater leisure. In one case, this resulted in the identification of a Roman inscribed funerary altar as one of the 'lost' marbles, once in the possession of Charles Townley, whose vast eighteenth-century collection of Graeco-Roman sculpture was purchased by Act of Parliament in 1805 and deposited in the British Museum.

A view of the exhibition in the Kiddell Gallery at Sotheby's, New Bond Street

From left to right: a Graeco-Roman marble torso of a youth, first century BC–first century AD (private collection); an Attic black-figure hydria, 530–520 BC (collection of Lt Col Sir Walter Bromley-Davenport TD, DL); an Attic red-figure column krater, *circa* 530 BC (Governors of Harrow School); an Attic black-figure hydria, *circa* 530 BC (private collection); a Roman marble hound, second century AD (private collection); an Attic black-figure neck amphora, *circa* 520 BC (private collection); an Attic marble head of a bearded man, fourth century BC (private collection); an Attic black-figure amphora, *circa* 525 BC (collection of Lt Col Sir Walter Bromley-Davenport, TD, DL)

Tribal art

A Maori gable peak figure (*teko teko*), New Zealand,
height 48½in (123.2cm)
New York $22,000 (£15,493). 15.XI.85

A Benin bronze plaque of a warrior chief with retainers, Nigeria, height 17¼in (44cm)
London £176,000 ($274,560). 23.VI.86

A La Tolita gold figure of a warrior, southern Ecuador, fifth century BC–sixth century AD,
height 9in (22.9cm)
New York $110,000 (£75,342). 26.XI.85

A Navajo chief's blanket,
Classic Period, Second Phase,
68in by 57½in
(172.7cm by 146cm)
New York $35,200 (£23,946)
30.V.86

A Zia oversized polychrome
jar, attributed to Trinidad
Medina, twentieth century,
height 25½in (64.8cm)
New York $22,000 (£14,966)
30.V.86

Islamic art

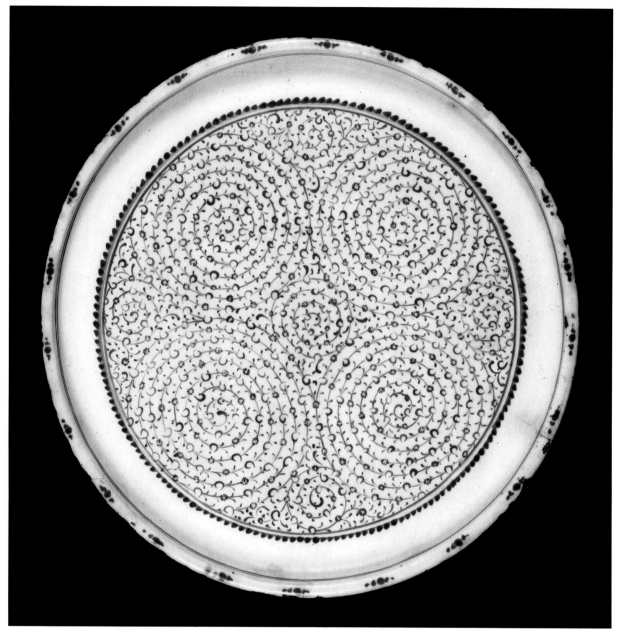

An Isnik 'Golden Horn' pottery dish, *circa* 1530, diameter 11⅛in (28.2cm)
London £33,000 ($51,150). 16.IV.86

Opposite
An Ottoman silver-gilt ewer, *circa* 1500, height 11in (27.9cm)
London £24,200 ($37,510). 16.IV.86

A Mamluk silver-inlaid brass bowl, mid fourteenth century, diameter 7in (17.8cm)
London £6,380 ($9,889). 16.IV.86

A Safavid open-work steel plaque, mid sixteenth century, length 15in (38cm)
London £36,300 ($53,724). 15.X.85

This plaque belongs to a group of eight. Each plaque bears a verse from a poem in Arabic
referring to The Fourteen Innocent Ones.

An Ottoman marquetry wood table set with an Isnik tile, mid sixteenth century,
diameter 2ft (61cm)
London £22,000 ($34,100). 16.IV.86

A Qajar oil painting of Fath-'Ali Shah, Ruler of Persia, attributed to
Mirza Baba, *circa* 1800, 69in by 41in (175cm by 104cm)
New York $41,250 (£28,061). 30.V.86

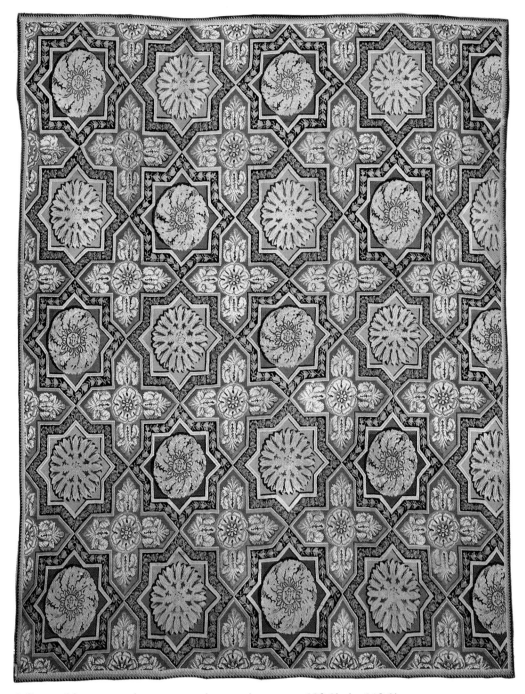

A Bessarabian carpet, last quarter nineteenth century, 18ft 9in by 14ft 9in
(571.5cm by 450cm)
New York $41,250 (£28,061). 31.V.86
From the collection of the late Elizabeth F. Cheney

A Salor wedding trapping, *circa* 1800, 7ft 4in by 2ft 6in (223.5cm by 76cm)
New York $67,100 (£45,646). 31.V.86
From the collection of the late Frances Fagley Coury

This trapping was woven by women of the Salor tribe to adorn a bride's camel on her wedding day. The Salor, a nomadic tribe, dominated Central Asia until their demise at the beginning of the nineteenth century.

Working within a traditional colour palette and design repertoire, evolving from Seljuk, Turkic and Chinese cloudcollar influences, the weaver has created a stunning design. The extraordinarily successful merging of the elements of the design and use of a great luxury of materials in this trapping was exceptional even for the Salor. It must have been created for someone important to warrant such expenditure of materials and labour.

One of a few known examples, this trapping has long been considered the pinnacle of Salor workmanship.

A Kashgar silk rug, *circa* 1800, 4ft 8in by 3ft 3in (142cm by 99cm)
New York $25,300 (£17,211). 31.V.86

A Faraghan silk rug, nineteenth century, 5ft 10in by 4ft 7in (178cm by 140cm)
London £22,000 ($34,100). 16.IV.86

A Malayer carpet, nineteenth century, 11ft 7in by 9ft 4in (353cm by 285cm)
London £20,900 ($32,395). 16.IV.86

Tang pottery

Margaret Medley

In the past there seem to have been three really colourful periods in Chinese history. To the splendid textiles of the Han dynasty (206 BC – AD 220), the Tang dynasty (AD 618 to 906) added brilliant pottery, made primarily for burial, and the Ming dynasty (AD 1368 to 1644), lacquer and cloisonné enamel. But it is the Tang pottery, with its polychrome glazes that is most striking, and the animals in particular on account of their realism. Some splendid examples were sold at Sotheby's this season (Fig. 1).

Prior to the Tang period pottery was extremely sombre, but the impact of foreign influences combined with a desire for novelty led to the brilliant use of fritted lead glazes that developed early in the seventh century. The potters began to explore a new aspect of their craft; the decorative use of colour patterning. Few Tang pieces display this better than the offering trays with their impressed designs, as may be seen in the two examples illustrated (Figs. 2 and 3), in which identical designs have been used. This particular design seems to have been popular, but by changing the arrangement of the colours, often using flat colour rather than dappling as in Fig. 3, a totally different impression of both design and dimensions of an object is conveyed, adding remarkable variety to what would otherwise be simply repetition.

Alongside this colourful treatment of surface there ran another current, which had always been present, but somewhat subdued; the sensuous appreciation of form combined with colour. The full rounded jar with blue glaze (Fig. 4) is a splendid example of this. The burgeoning shape is given added power by the sophisticated use of a thin double line at a critical point in the contour. This beguiles the eye into following round the vessel so that its mass and smoothness are visually experienced. One unusual point about this jar is that it is fully glazed inside with a colourless glaze, a rare occurrence in jars of this kind.

Combined with an interest in colour patterning and sensuousness is a delight in realism, best expressed in the horses, camels and attendant figures. The horse (Fig. 1), formerly in the Brodie Lodge collection, is a fine example of vigour of expression combined with excellent technical skill. Such pieces were assembled from moulded parts to which sculptural details and colour were added, only rarely overstepping the bounds of realism into fantasy. For that the goggle-eyed guardian figures make up a great deal. Two examples in the sale seem to have come from the same moulds so far as the main structure of the body is concerned, while the animal heads on the

Fig. 1
A *sancai* glazed pottery figure of a Fereghan horse, Tang Dynasty, height 25½in (64.8cm)
New York $506,000 (£341,892). 4.VI.86

Fig. 2
A *sancai* glazed tripod dish, Tang Dynasty, diameter 9⅜in (23.8cm)
London £14,300 ($22,451). 10.VI.86

shoulders have been differently treated. As was the normal practice at the time, the heads were made separately and luted into the neck slot. A common feature of these ferocious figures, and indeed common to all the human figures, is the fact that the heads were left unglazed and appropriate details painted in by hand after the firing. Guardians of this fantastic kind always have starting eyes and bristling eyebrows and whiskers. A somewhat choleric disposition is often imparted by the gaping mouth and reddish face, adding to the furious aspect.

Of a very different character is the charming, if rather stout prima donna-like figure with blue glazed robe from the former Mount Trust collection (Fig. 5). The smooth slightly vacuous face is typical of the mid-eighth century figures of women, reflecting the contemporary concept of feminine beauty. This seems to have been strongly influenced by the stature and bearing of the famous, or infamous concubine of the Emperor Ming-huang, Yang Guifei, who by all accounts was rather rotund. Her character left much to be desired, for she was both devious and ambitious, and was ultimately killed by the Emperor's bodyguard.

Closely related in date to this pottery figure is the extremely fine stone sculpture of a woman seated on a drum-stool. This is a good example of what the Tang

Fig.3
A *sancai* glazed tripod dish, Tang Dynasty, diameter 9½in (24cm)
London £52,800 ($82,896). 10.VI.86

craftsman was capable of achieving when working on a small object. Large stone sculpture always seems to have presented difficulties until this time, when the craftsmen finally mastered the technique of expressing volume on a large scale. There are a number of figures of this character together with a few pottery parallels, of which one is in the Museum of Far Eastern Antiquities, Stockholm, and another of a woman playing a harp is in the Cleveland Museum of Art. It is tempting to believe that since the figures are shown seated, as though playing musical instruments, there may have been sets of half a dozen or so in both pottery and stone. Both types are always exceptionally well finished, displaying artistry of the highest quality.

The Tang tombs were first excavated at the end of the nineteenth century, notably by Swedish railway engineers. Their discovery led to the formation of one of the first collections in the west, made by the then crown prince of Sweden (later Gustav V), an enthusiastic and knowledgeable connoisseur. It is only since the Great War that interest in the funerary pottery has become more widespread. As in all areas of the art market it is the most splendid pieces for which there is the greatest competition, and the Tang pottery sold by Sotheby's this summer is undoubtedly the finest ever to have appeared at auction.

Fig. 4
A blue-glazed pottery jar, Tang Dynasty, height 6⅜in (16.1cm)
London £33,000 ($51,810). 10.VI.86

Fig. 5, *opposite*
A blue-glazed figure of a court lady, Tang Dynasty, height 13⅞in (35.2cm)
London £203,500 ($319,495). 10.VI.86

Chinese art

An archaic bronze ritual food vessel and cover (*ding*), late Shang Dynasty,
height 7½in (19.1cm)
London £115,500 ($174,405). 10.XII.85

Opposite
An archaic bronze covered vessel (*fangyi*), late Shang Dynasty,
height 11¼in (28.6cm)
London £143,000 ($215,930). 10.XII.85

A stone figure of a female musician,
Tang Dynasty, height 16$\frac{7}{8}$in (43cm)
London £159,500 ($250,415). 10.VI.86

Opposite
A glazed pottery figure of a camel,
Tang Dynasty, height 32$\frac{5}{8}$in (83cm)
London £319,000 ($500,830). 10.VI.86

A glazed pottery figure of a polo player, Tang Dynasty, length 13¾in (35cm)
London £187,000 ($293,590). 10.VI.86

A gilt-bronze handle in the form of a dragon's
head, Han Dynasty, length 6¼in (15.9cm)
New York $38,500(£26,014). 4.VI.86

A gold melon shaped vessel, Song Dynasty,
height 5¼in (13.4cm)
New York $115,500(£78,041). 4.XII.85

A Ming blue and white wine cup (*yashou bei*), mark and period of Yongle, diameter 3⅝in (9.2cm)
London £363,000 ($569,910). 10.VI.86

A Yuan blue and white *meiping* and cover, third quarter fourteenth century, height 17¼in (44cm)
London £286,000 ($431,860). 10.XII.85

A celadon-ground *famille-rose* teapot and cover, seal mark and period of Qianlong,
height 5⅜in (13.7cm)
Hong Kong HK$550,000 (£46,374:$70,488). 20.V.86

An Imperial pink-ground *famille-rose* bowl, four character mark *Kangxi yuzhi*, and of the period, diameter 5¾in (14.7cm)
Hong Kong HK$495,000 (£41,737:$63,440). 20.V.86

An enamelled boar's head tureen, cover and stand, Qianlong, length $19\frac{5}{8}$in (49.9cm)
Monte Carlo FF666,000 (£61,953:$93,147). 23.VI.86

A cock tureen, cover and stand, bearing the arms of Bermúdez of Galicia, 1770–80,
length 19⅝in (49.9cm)
New York $96,250 (£68,262). 31.I.86

An armorial basin made for the Portuguese market and decorated with the arms of Teixeira and Mello, early eighteenth century, diameter 22¼in (56.5cm)
Monte Carlo FF610,500 (£56,791:$85,385). 23.VI.86

Opposite
A Ming rhinoceros horn ewer and cover, possibly fifteenth century, four character seal mark *Yuan Shangqing zhi*, height 7¾in (19.8cm)
Hong Kong HK$462,000 (£38,954:59,211). 20.V.86

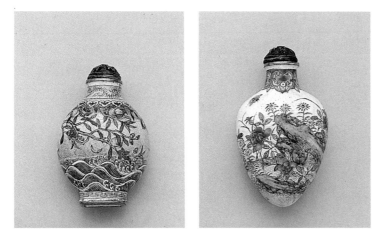

A boxed set of two Peking enamel snuff bottles, Qianlong, one
bearing a four character mark of the period
New York $35,200(£23,624). 2.XII.85
From the collection of Dr Paula Hallett

An enamelled glass snuff bottle by
Ye Family Workshops, Peking,
1933–43, four character mark
of Qianlong
London £9,020 ($14,342). 6.V.86
From the collection of
J.T. Wakefield

A jade bangle
Hong Kong HK$1,045,000
(£94,144:$133,685). 19.XI.85

Opposite
A suite of jade and diamond
jewellery comprising a necklace, a
pair of pendent earrings and a ring
Hong Kong HK$2,860,000
(£257,658:$365,874). 19.XI.85

Ding Yunpeng
SWEEPING THE ELEPHANT
Hanging scroll, ink and colour
on paper, signed, dated 1604,
with three seals of the artist,
49½in by 19½in
(125.7cm by 49.5cm)
New York $55,000 (£36,913)
3.VI.86

Anonymous

PORTRAIT OF HU ER CHA BA
Ink and colour on silk, with an
attached inscription in Chinese and
Manchu, dated 1760, and with one
seal of the Qianlong Emperor, *Qian
Long Yu Lan Zhi Bao*, 78¾in by 39⅜in
(200cm by 100cm)
New York $115,500 (£77,517)
3.VI.86

Hu Er Cha Ba was an Imperial
bodyguard of the first rank. This
portrait is one of a set of fifty
commissioned by the Emperor and
presented to his bodyguards.

Hua Yan, Xu Bin, Yan Yue, Zheng Xie

SPARROWS, CHRYSANTHEMUM, BAMBOO AND
ROCK

Hanging scroll, ink and colour on paper,
signed *Xinluo Shanren Hua Yan*, inscribed and
dated 1746, with seals of the artists,
43⅞in by 12in (111.5cm by 30.5cm)
New York $110,000 (£74,324). 5.XII.85
From the Yuzhai Collection

Gao Qifeng
IN HARMONY
Hanging scroll, ink and colour on paper, signed,
dated 1927, with two seals of the artist,
51in by 18⅜in (129.5cm by 46.7cm)
Hong Kong HK$209,000 (£17,622:$26,786). 22.V.86

Japanese art

A Namban lacquer travelling shrine, Momoyama period, *circa* 1600, framing a contemporary painting on copper of the Holy Family with Saint John the Baptist, probably Spanish, height 24½in (62.3cm)
London £121,000 ($179,080). 12.XI.85

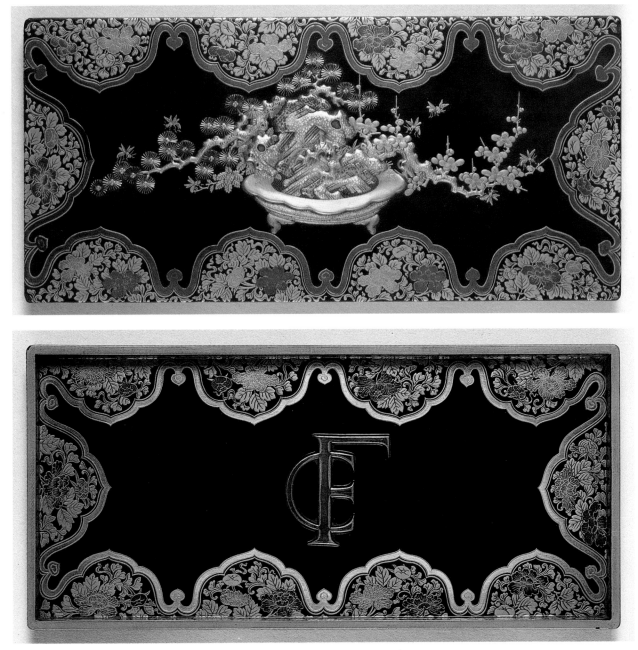

A lacquer box and cover, bearing the monogram *CF*, *circa* 1640, length 8⅜in (21.4cm)
London £28,600 ($45,760). 13.VI.86

A Kakiemon dish, second half seventeenth century,
diameter 12⅜in (31.4cm)
London £15,400 ($24,640). 13.VI.86

An early Kakiemon-style bottle, third quarter
seventeenth century, height 9⅝in (24.3cm)
London £14,300 ($22,022). 13.III.86

Utamaro
THE COURTESAN HANAZUMA OF HYOGOYA
WRINGING A LETTER
Oban, one from a set of prints entitled *A Comparison of the Outstanding Beauties of the Day*, signed
London £8,250 ($13,200). 13.VI.86

An earthenware vase by Kinkozan, signed with impressed mark, the panels by Sozan, signed, Meiji period, height 25⅜in (64.5cm)
London £16,500 ($24,420). 12.XI.85

An ivory *netsuke* of a tiger by
Otoman, signed, Hakata,
nineteenth century
London £12,100 ($17,908)
13.XI.85

An ivory *netsuke* of a rat by
Okatomo, signed, Kyoto,
eighteenth century
London £8,250 ($12,540) 20.II.86

An ivory *netsuke* of a *kirin* by
Tomotada, signed, Kyoto, eighteenth
century
London £19,800 ($30,096)
20.II.86

An ivory *netsuke* of a rat by
Masanao, signed, Kyoto,
eighteenth century
London £20,900 ($30,932)
13.XI.85

A kakiwood *netsuke* of a frog on a *kohone* leaf by Seiyodo Bunshojo,
signed, Iwami, late eighteenth – early nineteenth century
London £18,700 ($27,676). 13.XI.85

A bronze figure of a warrior priest by Suzuki Masayoshi, signed, Meiji period,
overall height 62¼in (158cm)
London £28,600 ($45,760). 12.VI.86

A moriage enamel vase by Ando Jubei, stamped and
with the artist's inlaid seal, late Meiji period,
height 11in (28cm)
London £15,400 ($23,716). 13.III.86

A cloisonné enamel vase by Namikawa Yasuyuki,
signed, Meiji period, height 7⅛in (18cm)
London £11,000 ($16,940). 13.III.86

An ivory figure of a hunter by Ishikawa Komei, signed, Meiji period, height 15in (38cm)
London £20,900 ($32,186). 13.III.86

Ando Hiroshige
MORNING GLORIES, GRASSHOPPER AND BAMBOO
One from a set of prints entitled *Flowers of the Four Seasons*, 9¼in by 11½in
(23.4cm by 29.4cm)
New York $16,500 (£11,538). 6.XI.85
From the collection of Salvatore J. Tarantino

Hiroshige II

VIEWS OF THE PROVINCES

Oban tate-e album with seventy-seven prints from the series *The Hundred Views of the Provinces*, signed, dated 1859, 1860, 1861 or 1864, with six prints from the series *The Souvenirs of Edo*, signed, dated 1861
New York $57,750 (£40,385). 7.XI.85

Opposite

Anonymous

NAMBAN SHIP AND FIGURES

Six-fold screen, ink, colours, gold and silver on paper, Tokugawa period, late eighteenth century, each panel 58¾in by 23⅜in (149.3cm by 59.4cm)
New York $20,900 (£14,615). 7.XI.85

Postage stamps

India, 1858 envelope from Bangalore to London, bearing 1854 4a Head Die III, Frame Die II, vertical pair
London £3,300 ($4,917). 19.XI.85
From the collection of The Rt. Hon Lord Home of the Hirsel, KT

France, 1854 entire letter from Charles Thomas Clifford to his brother, Lord Clifford, in Italy, bearing 1849–52 1f carmine pair
London £5,775 ($8,605). 19.XI.85
From the collection of The Lord Clifford of Chudleigh

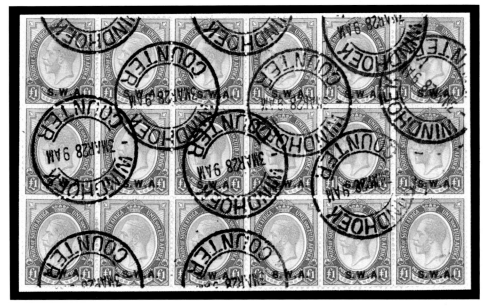

South West Africa, 1927–30 £1 block of eighteen with Windhoek Counter
cancellations
Johannesburg R8,500 (£2,758:$3,842). 15.VIII.85

Norway, 1864 outer wrapper from Sarpsborg to London, 84 skilling rate
London £6,600 ($9,834). 19.XI.85

Scientific instruments and the Arthur Frank Collection

Gerard L'E. Turner

It is remarkable that a sale of old scientific instruments should rate an article in the British Airways inflight magazine, *High Life*. Paintings, silver, porcelain, yes, but scientific instruments are relative newcomers on the collecting scene. Yet the Arthur Frank collection, sold by Sotheby's on 25 March 1986, achieved such celebrity. How has this come about?

During the nineteenth century, European collectors of wrought metal work included astrolabes, some types of sundial, and metal globes on elaborate stands among their treasures. But their inclusion was incidental; the instruments being viewed purely as *objets d'art*. Probably the first knowledgeable collector who had some clear objective in his concentration on scientific instruments was Lewis Evans, brother of the famous archaeologist, Sir Arthur Evans. He amassed a large collection in the 1890s and 1900s. It was a fortunate chance which led to a meeting between Lewis Evans and Robert Gunther, the first archaeologist of science, a man who was uniquely able to recognise the historical importance of such a collection, and was in the process of establishing a museum, as part of Oxford University. Immediately after the end of the First World War, Gunther arranged a special exhibition in the Bodleian Library at Oxford of instruments he had discovered in the colleges of the university. This brought Gunther and Evans together, and in due course the latter's collection was given to the university, and housed in the top floor of the Old Ashmolean building in Broad Street. On 5 May 1925, Gunther's vision took permanent form, first as the Lewis Evans Collection, and ten years later as the Museum of the History of Science.

An earlier impetus towards the collection of scientific instruments had come with the great *Special Loan Collection of Scientific Apparatus* at the South Kensington Museum in 1876, which included items discovered in Britain, and borrowed from all over the world. Here the main emphasis was on current achievement in precision instrument-making, but each section included a small historical element, tracing the development of a given class of instrument. It was this collection, intended to stimulate scientific education, from which the Science Museum in London was created some thirty years later. But Gunther's unique achievement was his dedication to the concept of preserving the scientific instruments of the past, what might be described as the Noah instinct. This is the driving principle, conscious or unconscious, of the serious collector.

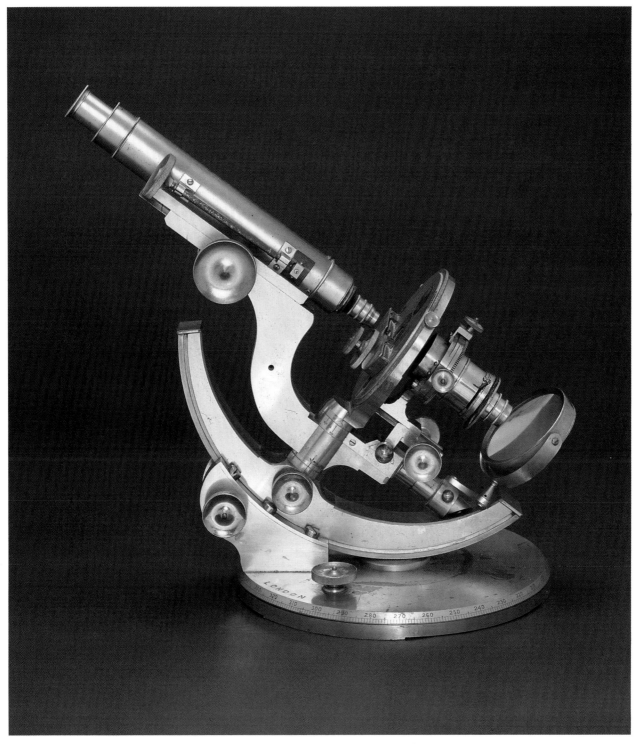

Fig. 1
A Ross-Wenham brass radial compound monocular microscope, London, stamped *Ross London 5399*, 1880, height 16⅜in (41cm)
London £4,620 ($7,207). 25.III.86
From the collection of Arthur Frank

The twentieth century is the age of the specialist collector, not only of established art objects but of other artefacts, such as treen, bottles, playing cards, fans, to name only a few categories. Specialism also affected the scientific instrument field. The Belgian, Max Elskamp, formed an elegant collection of sundials at the turn of the nineteenth century, now housed in a museum in Liège. The nucleus of the History of Science Museum at Cambridge University, founded in 1944, was the personal collection of Robert S. Whipple, chairman and managing director of the Cambridge Instrument Company, a man who valued the skills embodied in old instruments: ideas made brass. At the same date, the Oxford museum acquired a magnificent optical collection, the microscopes, telescopes and some other instruments of Dr Reginald Clay. These are just a few of the bequests and acquisitions of personal collections that have enriched science museums in Britain and on the Continent, making possible over the past thirty years the academic study of the development of scientific instruments. This in turn has greatly benefited collectors, who can get sound advice from museum staff, and can learn about the historical context of the items they collect. The resulting stimulus to this field has meant that three leading auction houses now hold quarterly specialist sales of scientific instruments, attracting buyers from all over the world to London as the pre-eminent centre. In the spring of 1983, all the dramatis personae of this thriving market were brought together by the foundation of the Scientific Instrument Society, which enables auctioneers, museum staff, dealers and collectors to meet in a club-like atmosphere. It would not, perhaps, be too far-fetched to trace these developments back to the austere and dedicated figure of Robert Gunther.

Among the energetic collectors of the immediate post-war period was Mr Arthur Frank. His father was an instrument maker and retailer in Glasgow, and in the cellar of his shop accumulated the nucleus of a collection to which the son added over many years. Parts of it have already been made over through an amalgam of sale and gift to the National Museum of Photography, Film and Television at Bradford (an annexe of the Science Museum, London), and to the Royal Museum of Scotland. It was the remainder that was sold at Sotheby's.

The items on sale included marine chronometers, navigational instruments, sundials, quadrants, surveying instruments, telescopes (reflecting and refracting), spyglasses and above all, microscopes. Of the nine instruments that achieved top prices, eight were optical instruments, and all but one of these microscopes, among them a rare Ross radial microscope (Fig. 1). Comparatively few of this model were made, as the design by Francis Wenham was felt by many to be needlessly complicated. The star of the sale was a John Marshall microscope (Fig. 2, *centre*). There are probably a couple of dozen microscopes in gold-tooled leather by this maker in the world, and two in the Oxford museum. Far more exquisite and rare in my view was the 'New Universal Double Microscope' by George Adams Senior, with a turned ivory body tube mounted over a wheel of seven objectives, which, complete in its box, was the best preserved I have ever seen. The next two most coveted instruments were Culpeper-type microscopes (Fig. 2, *left and right*) of

Fig. 2, *from left to right*
A second-form Culpeper compound monocular microscope by Thomas Ribright, London, signed, *circa* 1740, height 16⅛in (41cm), £6,600 ($10,296)
A compound monocular microscope by John Marshall, London, *circa* 1715, height 18⅞in (48cm), £25,850 ($40,326)
A Scarlett-form Culpeper microscope, English, *circa* 1730, height 15⅜in (39cm), £10,450 ($16,300)

The scientific instruments illustrated on this page are from the collection of Arthur Frank and were sold in London on 25 March 1986.

the mid-eighteenth century, followed by a John Cuff of the same period, and a very neat, small sextant signed by Ramsden, of *circa* 1790. Jesse Ramsden, who died in 1800, was the greatest of the London makers of the later eighteenth century and made the instruments for the national surveys of England, France and North America. The Cuff microscope and the sextant fetched £5,280, a lucernal microscope signed W & S Jones, £4,950, and a most exotic telescope £4,620, more than twice its estimated price. This was a richly decorated Japanese instrument with five draw-tubes, opening to three meters length. When closed, it fitted into a presentation case of black, red and gold lacquer. A similar instrument, also obviously made in Japan in the early nineteenth century, is in the Oxford museum. These were the highlights among 341 lots, whose hammer prices totalled around £300,000.

Collectors' sales

A Louis XV microscope by Alexis Magny, *circa* 1750, height 19¼in (49cm)
Monte Carlo FF843,600 (£81,903:$119,490). 23.II.86

An English brass universal equinoctial dial by
Augustine Ryther, signed and dated *1588*,
diameter $2\frac{1}{8}$in (5.5cm)
London £17,600 ($26,400). 23.X.85

A European planispheric astrolabe, *circa* 1300
London £31,900 ($50,402). 18.VI.86

Left
A French doll by Casimir Bru, the bisque head and
shoulders incised *BRU Jne. 9*, *circa* 1875,
height 24⅜in (62cm)
London £11,000 ($15,840). 5.II.86

Below
A German character doll by Kammer and Reinhardt,
the bisque head incised *106K*R53*, *circa* 1909,
height 22½in (58cm)
London £24,200 ($38,720). 20.V.86

Opposite, left to right
A French beaded *crêpe de chine* cocktail dress,
by Jean Patou, *circa* 1930
London £4,620 ($7,392). 20.V.86
A French chiffon beaded cocktail dress, possibly by
Jean Patou, 1925–30
London £2,200 ($3,520). 20.V.86

A German tinplate steam car, probably by Carette, *circa* 1898, length 9in (22.9cm)
London £13,750 ($22,000). 20.V.86

James Bond's Aston Martin from the film *Goldfinger*, 1963
New York $275,000 (£179,739). 28.VI.86

A French musical automaton of a negro smoking by Gustave Vichy, *circa* 1880, height 24in (61cm)
London £9,680 ($14,133). 1.X.85

A 1906 Renault 14/20hp Type X single landaulette, with coachwork by Hooper & Co.
Ludlow £33,000 ($53,460). 5.VII.86
From the collection of the late E.W. Pilkington

A 1910 Rolls-Royce 40/50hp Silver Ghost five-seater Roi-Des-Belges replica tourer with
twenty-four carat gold-plated fittings, with coachwork by Wilkinsons of Derby
Monte Carlo FF2,830,500 (£257,318:$385,102). 25.V.86

A 1932 Bugatti Type 55 super sport roadster
London (Honourable Artillery Company) £440,000 ($673,200). 9.XII.85

Photograph courtesy of Neill Bruce, Midland Motor Museum

A 1933 Alfa Romeo 8C 2300 supercharged Le Mans sports tourer, uprated to 2.6 litres, with
coachwork by Carosserie Touring of Milan
Monte Carlo FF2,386,500 (£216,955:$324,694). 25.V.86

Wine

A silver-plated decanting cradle, French, late nineteenth century
London £1,078 ($1,703). 28.V.86

Château Lafite 1806, CB (one bottle)
London £10,780 ($16,170). 11.XII.85

In the season ending July 1986, wine sales held by Sotheby's world-wide totalled £2,845,844 ($4,126,474). It was one of the most active years since the department's foundation in 1970.

The majority of the twenty-one wine sales were held in London, although there were a few important sales at our new premises at Summers Place, Billingshurst, West Sussex. Overseas sales centres included Geneva, Johannesburg and Tokyo. Only two wine sales have ever been held in Japan. The first was last year's Sotheby's sale. The highly sensitive Japanese market had responded badly to the news of the Austrian 'antifreeze' scandal and there had been heavy falls in wine imports. This, however, did not appear to affect the excellent result of the sale. In Johannesburg the inaugural sale of the Cape Independent Winemakers' Guild was highly successful with a capacity attendance buying some of the finest and most individual wines the Cape can produce. In addition, David Molyneux-Berry was the guest auctioneer at the Fourth Annual Detroit International Wine Auction, which raised a record total in aid of the Detroit Community Music School.

Significant sales in London included a spectacular range of rare vintage Armagnac, generously donated by the producers in aid of the Ordre Souverain de Malte, and a unique selection of vintages of Château Lanessan, the well known but unclassified property in Cussac adjoining St Julien in the Médoc.

Left to right
Château Lanessan 1900, CB (one magnum), London £352 ($556). 28.V.86
Tokaji Aszú Cabinet Wein, OB (one half litre), London £121 ($185). 26.III.86
Grand Bas Armagnac Garreau 1942, OB (one bottle), London £116 ($173). 11.XII.85
A John Loach 1844 patent corkscrew, London £825 ($1,304). 28.V.86
A Henry Shrapnel 1839 patent corkscrew, London £1,650 ($2,475). 11.XII.85

A number of items achieved noteworthy prices in London this season. These included six magnums of Château Pétrus 1961 CB £9,020 ($13,530); a dozen bottles of Château d'Yquem 1943 CB £1,430 ($2,145); a dozen bottles of Cockburn 1927 £1,012 ($1,599); a bottle of Madeira 1785 £242 ($370); and a bottle of Cognac Napoléon, Impériale, Grande Fine Champagne 1811 £264 ($396). In Tokyo a bottle of Romanée Conti 1937 made Y605,000 (£2,017:$3,005). There were also four sales of collectors' items including corkscrews, decanting cradles, old catalogues, antique bottles and wine bills. These sales generated considerable interest and many high prices were achieved.

A series of tastings tutored by the proprietors was held at the London Wine Trade Fair in May with ranges of wine from Châteaux Beychevelle, Brane Cantenac, La Louvière and Vieux Certan. In addition, the continuing series of wine evenings has been well attended, covering such subjects as 1978 Vintage First Growth Clarets, Red Burgundy, Fine Italian Wines, Vintage Port, Rhône and Australian Wine.

This autumn Sotheby's Publications will add *Champagne* by Tom Stevenson to their series of wine books. *Champagne* is the first major new work on the subject to be published in English for nearly twenty years and provides a comprehensive account of the region, its wines and producers. Future titles in the series will cover the wines of the Graves and Chianti.

'Rule, Britannia!'

Britain's marine heritage was commemorated at Sotheby's annual Christmas exhibition, held in association with the Royal National Lifeboat Institution. More than 300 pictures, works of art and other objects representing Britain's proudest achievements in time of war, nautical science, discovery and rescue were exhibited.

The dawn of Britain's mastery of the seas was charted with a display of artifacts from the jewel of Henry VIII's fleet, the *Mary Rose*, raised from the seabed in 1982, over 400 years after she sank off Portsmouth. Among the earliest works in the exhibition was the Armada portrait of Queen Elizabeth I, radiantly attired in a jewelled court dress, painted to commemorate the defeat of the Spanish Armada in 1588. Portraits of high-ranking admirals through four centuries were displayed and a separate section was devoted to the most famous of them all, Horatio Nelson, hero of Trafalgar and the most successful tactician in the history of naval warfare. His full-length portrait by Sir William Beechey (see opposite) dominated the southern wall of the main gallery. Displayed with the painting were his collar of the Most Honourable Order of the Bath, the telescope given to him when he joined his uncle's ship at the age of twelve and his pocket book, which was in his possession at the time of his death.

Paintings chronicling the maritime rivalry in the latter part of the seventeenth century between the two great trading nations, the Dutch and English, were loaned from private collections, many of them for the first time. There was also fine silver, documents and artifacts to illustrate the history of some of Britain's greatest naval commanders, portraits of whom by Gainsborough, Reynolds, Hoare and Copley, among others, were exhibited. There was also a portrait by Thomas Hudson of the notorious *Hon. John Byng, Admiral of the Blue* who was court-martialled and shot for abandoning Minorca to the French.

Mindful of the purpose of the exhibition, the paintings, drawings, models and medals in the final gallery told the story of the bravery of the lifeboat men. Organised coastal lifesaving is comparatively recent and dates from the legendary heroism of such figures as Grace Darling who, in 1838, rescued survivors of the *Forfarshire*, wrecked in heavy seas between Hull and Dundee. All the exhibits were generously lent by members and supporters of the RNLI, and proceeds from the sale of the exhibition catalogue were donated to the Institution, as a contribution to the men and women who risk their lives to save others from the sea.

Sir William Beechey, RA
VISCOUNT NELSON, VICE-ADMIRAL OF THE WHITE (1758–1805)
Circa 1801, 102in by 72in (259cm by 183cm)

Notes on contributors

Dr Keith Andrews was, until recently, Keeper of Prints and Drawings at the National Gallery of Scotland. He has published catalogues of the Italian drawings (1968) and the Netherlandish drawings (1985) in the National Gallery's collection. He is also the author of *The Nazarenes* (1964) and *Adam Elsheimer* (1977), an enlarged German edition of which was published in Munich in 1985.

Mary Black is the former director and curator of both the Abby Aldrich Rockefeller Folk Art Center in Williamsburg, Virginia, and the Museum of American Folk Art, New York City, where she is currently consulting curator for special projects. She has organised more than a hundred major exhibitions of American art. She is the author of numerous books and articles on American folk art, old New York photography and American advertising art.

Carol Eaton Hevner is at present engaged in research for the National Gallery of Art, Washington, DC, on Rembrandt Peale's technical treatise *Notes of the Painting Room*. The manuscript belongs to the Historical Society of Pennsylvania where she was curator of an exhibition of Peale in 1985.

Dr Rosamund McKitterick is a fellow of Newnham College, Cambridge where she lectures on early medieval history and, until recently, on medieval Latin palaeography. In addition to writing a number of specialist articles she is the author of *The Frankish Church and the Carolingians 751–987* (1983). A catalogue of the medieval manuscripts in the Pepys Library, Magdalene College, Cambridge is in production and she is at present engaged on *The Carolingians and the Written Word*.

Fanny Mallary was formerly in the Books and Manuscripts department of Sotheby's, New York, where she catalogued the sale of Redouté's *Les Liliacées*. She now works at Dartmouth College Library, New Hampshire, and is co-author, with her husband Peter Mallary, of a book on Redouté to be published later this year.

Margaret Medley was formerly curator of the Percival David Foundation of Chinese Art in the University of London, and Honorary Lecturer on Chinese art in the School of Oriental and African Studies. She is the author of *The Chinese Potter* (1976), *Yuan Porcelain and Stoneware* (1974), *T'ang Pottery and Porcelain* (1981), as well as numerous articles on Chinese art subjects.

Dr Carlos Picón was formerly a junior research fellow at Christ Church College, Oxford, and assistant curator of the Ashmole Archive at King's College, London. He is at present curator of Western Antiquities at the San Antonio Museum of Art in Texas. He has recently completed a catalogue of archaic Greek sculptures from Ephesus for the British Museum.

Graham Reynolds was Keeper of Prints and Drawings, and Paintings at the Victoria & Albert Museum, London from 1959–74. His most recent publications are the *Catalogue of the Miniatures in the Wallace Collection* (1980), *The Later Paintings and Drawings of John Constable* (1984). His *English Portrait Miniatures* (1952), is to be reprinted in 1987.

Richard Thomson lectures in the history of art at the university of Manchester where he is a specialist in late nineteenth-century art. In addition to publishing a number of articles in this field he is the author of *Toulouse-Lautrec* (1977), *French Nineteenth-Century Drawings in the Whitworth Art Gallery* (1981), *Seurat* (1985) and, with Christopher Lloyd, *Impressionist Drawings* (1986).

Guy M. Wilson has worked in the Royal Armouries for the past fourteen years, latterly as Keeper of Edged Weapons and then Keeper of Firearms and Deputy Master. He has written and lectured widely on arms and armour and related subjects. He is a fellow of the Society of Antiquaries of London.

Dr Gerard L'E. Turner has been a curator at the Museum of the History of Science, Oxford, for over twenty years. His most recent publications include *Antique Scientific Instruments* (1980), *Essays on the History of the Microscope* (1980) and *Nineteenth-Century Scientific Instruments* (1983). He is Chairman of the Scientific Instrument Society.

The following contributors are experts at Sotheby's: John Culme (London); John L. Tancock (New York).

A Worcester candlestick figure of a gardener, 1770–80, height 8⅝in (22cm)
London £10,450 ($16,720). 1.VII.86
From the Rous Lench Collection

Index

A white marble fountain, *circa* 1880, height 97in (246.4cm)
Billingshurst £31,900 ($50,402). 28.V.86

ART AT AUCTION
The year at Sotheby's 1985–86

SOTHEBY'S PUBLICATIONS

© Sotheby's 1986

First published for Sotheby's Publications by
Philip Wilson Publishers Ltd,
26 Litchfield Street, London WC2H 9NJ
and
Sotheby's Publications,
Harper & Row, Publishers, Inc.,
10 East 53rd Street, New York, NY 10022

ISBN 0 85667 323 4
ISSN 0084–6783
Library of Congress Catalog Card Number 67 30652

Editors: Georgia Fogg, Louise Berg
Assistant Editors: Lisa Wortley, Susan Rosenfeld
Assistant (New York): Elizabeth White

Design: Mary Osborne
Printed in England by Jolly & Barber Ltd, Rugby, Warwickshire,
and bound by Dorstel Press Ltd, Harlow, Essex

Note
Prices given throughout this book include the buyer's premium applicable in the saleroom concerned.
These prices are shown in the currency in which they were realised. The sterling and dollar
equivalent figures, shown in brackets, are based on the rates of exchange on the day of sale.

Sotheby's galleries at New Bond Street, Bloomfield Place and Conduit Street are indicated by the
designation 'London', and those at York Avenue by the designation 'New York'.

Frontispiece
Andrea Mantegna
THE HOLY FAMILY WITH SAINTS ELIZABETH AND JOHN THE BAPTIST
Tempera on linen, 23⅝in by 19½in (60cm by 49.5cm)
Monte Carlo FF17,760,000 (£1,652,093:$2,483,916). 21.VI.86

Endpaper – front
Beatrix Potter
Detail of a sheet of preparatory watercolour drawings for Edward Lear's *The Owl and the Pussy Cat*
London £9,350 ($14,773). 20.VI.86

Endpaper – back
Ernest Shepard
Brownie, Disobedience, If I were King, Rice Pudding and *The Three Foxes*, from the complete set of
preliminary pencil drawings for A.A. Milne's *When We Were Very Young*, with the author's original
pencil drafts for thirty-eight poems, the printer's working typescript, correspondence and copies
of the book and other related publications, *circa* 1924
London £132,000 ($212,520). 10.VII.86
From the collection of the Carl H. Pforzheimer Library

Contents

Jacques-Louis David

SKETCHBOOK EXECUTED IN ROME

One of ninety-eight studies in pen, ink and wash with pencil, sketchbook numbered *11*, *circa* 1780
Monte Carlo FF1,720,500 (£167,039:$243,697). 22.II.86

David executed twelve large sketchbooks during the time he spent in Rome, after winning the Prix de Rome in 1774. As soon as he arrived in Italy, he felt that his work up to that time had been misguided. He stopped painting altogether and began drawing prolifically, copying the works of Classical Antiquity and the Old Masters, sketching the city and everything he found there.

Preface

A. Alfred Taubman
Chairman, Sotheby's Holdings, Inc.

The 1985–86 auction season reflects the continuing development of an international art market, a market increasingly supported by private collectors seeking the world's finest works of art and jewelry. This edition of *Art at Auction* chronicles the season's most significant events, including the sales of Rembrandt Peale's powerful portrait, *Rubens Peale with a geranium*; the Empress Josephine's copy of Redouté's masterwork, *Les Liliacées*; the magnificent jewels of Countess Mona Bismarck; superb English porcelain from the Rous Lench collection; Flemish paintings and important French furniture from the collection of Charles De Pauw.

We are proud to offer our clients a broad range of professional services. Our experts, dedicated and talented men and women, have developed extraordinary connoisseurship and an intimate knowledge of the market. Periodically, their research leads to the identification of important works of art, hitherto unknown to scholars. Recent examples include the discovery of *The Holy Family*, an unrecorded painting by Mantegna, and the emergence of an unpublished Carolingian Gospel Book dating from the ninth century. These works sold for record prices this season in our auction rooms in Monte Carlo and London.

As an increasing number of collectors visit Sotheby's, we are taking steps to ensure that our auction facilities remain the finest in the world. We have announced expansion plans for our New York galleries, and are restoring our landmark buildings on Bond Street, including a special gallery named in honour of the late Peter Wilson. As a further resource for collectors, Sotheby's now conducts extensive educational programs on both sides of the Atlantic.

I would like to take this opportunity to welcome three exceptional individuals to Sotheby's. The Rt. Hon the Earl of Gowrie, who served as Minister for the Arts from 1983–85, will in January assume the position of Chairman of Sotheby's United Kingdom. In addition, Charles D. Atwood has been named President and Chief Executive Officer of Sotheby's International Realty Corporation, an organisation that increasingly is becoming an important resource for our auction clients. Simon de Pury, the distinguished Director of the Thyssen Collection in Lugano has joined the firm as Chairman of Sotheby's Switzerland and Managing Director of Sotheby's in Europe. Lord Gowrie and Messrs de Pury and Atwood join our

Pieter Brueghel the Younger
THE BIRD'S NESTER
On panel, inscribed *P. Brevghel*, 14in by 19in (36cm by 48.5cm)
London £242,000 ($370,260). 9.IV.86
From the collection of the late Charles De Pauw

senior international management team of Michael L. Ainslie, President and Chief Executive Officer of Sotheby's Holdings, Inc., Julian Thompson, Chairman of Sotheby's International, Timothy D. Llewellyn, Managing Director of Sotheby's UK, and John L. Marion, Chairman, and Diana D. Brooks, Executive Vice President of Sotheby's North America. Of course, all Sotheby's programs are greatly enhanced by the participation and support of the Board of Directors of Sotheby's Holdings, Inc. I take great personal pride in my association with them and am pleased to acknowledge the vital role they play in Sotheby's ongoing success.

Paintings and drawings

Cristoforo di Giovanni da Sanseverino and Angelo da Camerino
THE VIRGIN AND CHILD ENTHRONED WITH ANGELS AND DONORS
Tempera and gold leaf on panel, signed, inscribed and dated 1457, 68⅛in by 27½in (173cm by 70cm)
Florence L214,700,000 (£92,265:$142,088)
14.IV.86

This picture was originally at the centre of an altarpiece commissioned in 1457 by Jacopo di San Ginesio, a physician at the papal court.

Opposite
Pseudo-Pier Francesco Fiorentino
THE VIRGIN AND CHILD
Tempera on panel, 28¾in by 18½in (73cm by 47cm)
London £159,500 ($244,035). 9.IV.86

Adriaen Isenbrandt
THE VIRGIN AND CHILD SEATED ON A DAIS
On panel, 12½in by 9in (31.8cm by 22.9cm)
New York $170,500 (£113,667). 5.VI.86

Jan de Beer
THE ADORATION OF THE MAGI
On panel, 24¾in by 20in (63cm by 50.9cm)
New York $187,000 (£130,769). 17.I.86

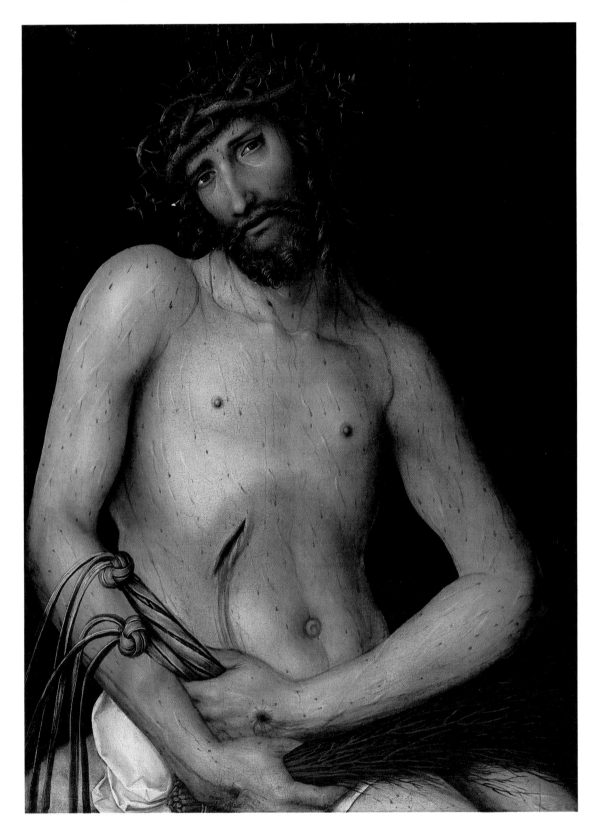

Pieter Brueghel the Younger
PEASANTS DANCING AROUND A MAYPOLE
On panel transferred to canvas, signed or inscribed *P. Brevghel 16 . .*, 20in by 29½in (51cm by 75cm)
London £352,000 ($538,560). 9.IV.86
From the collection of the late Charles De Pauw

Opposite
Lucas Cranach the Elder
MAN OF SORROWS
On panel, signed with the artist's device, 31in by 22¼in (78.7cm by 56.5cm)
New York $214,500 (£150,000). 17.I.86
From the collection of the late Dr Paul Weiden

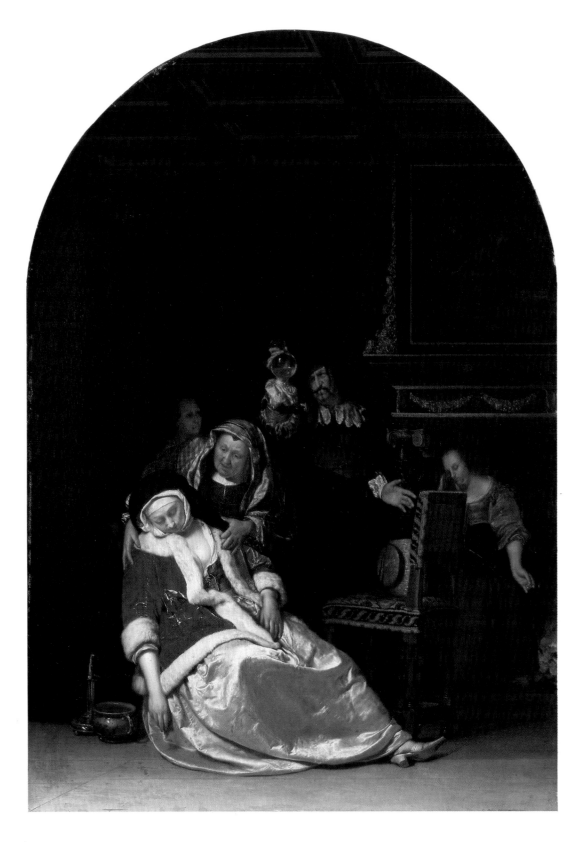

Meindert Hobbema
THE WATER-MILL
On panel, signed and dated *1662*, 23½in by 33in (59.5cm by 84cm)
New York $132,000 (£92,308). 17.I.86

Opposite
Frans van Mieris the Elder
THE DOCTOR'S VISIT
On panel, signed and dated *1667*, 17¼in by 12⅝in (44cm by 32cm)
Monte Carlo FF3,552,000 (£330,419:$496,783). 21.VI.86

Giovanni Francesco Barbieri, called Guercino
THE DENIAL OF SAINT PETER
Circa 1646, 54⅛in by 69½in (137.5cm by 176.5cm)
London £638,000 ($957,000). 11.XII.85

Giovanni Martinelli
THE JUDGMENT OF SOLOMON
57½in by 80½in (146cm by 204.5cm)
New York $170,500 (£119,231). 17.I.86

Sebastiano Ricci
VENUS AND ADONIS
41¾in by 59⅝in (105cm by 151.5cm)
Monte Carlo FF1,443,000 (£134,233:$201,818). 21.VI.86

Opposite
Luca Giordano
LUCRETIA
47¼in by 37⅜in (120cm by 95cm)
London £104,500 ($168,245). 2.VII.86

Giovanni Paolo Panini
A CLASSICAL SCENE WITH FIGURES MAKING AN OFFERING TO AESCULAPIUS ON THE TIBERINE ISLAND
Signed and dated 1734, 40⅛in by 36¼in (102cm by 92cm)
London £104,500 ($156,750). 11.XII.85

Antonio Canale, called Canaletto
THE ENTRANCE TO THE GRAND CANAL LOOKING TOWARDS THE BACINO, VENICE
42½in by 53½in (108cm by 136cm)
London £528,000 ($792,000). 11.XII.85
From the collection of the late W. A. Shand

Anne Vallayer-Coster
STILL LIFE WITH A VASE OF FLOWERS AND FRUIT
Signed and dated *M. Vallayer Coster an 8^m*, 25$\frac{3}{8}$in by 21in (64.5cm by 53.5cm)
Monte Carlo FF1,776,000 (£172,427:$251,558). 22.II.86

Hubert Robert
FIGURES BEFORE THE RUINS OF A ROMAN COLONNADE
Signed, 137¾in by 108¼in (350cm by 275cm)
Monte Carlo FF999,000 (£92,930:$139,720). 21.VI.86

The Springell Collection

Keith Andrews

The old master drawings sold in London this summer were the remainder of the collection formed over roughly fifty years by the late Dr Francis Springell and his wife. A substantial group of fifty-four drawings had already been auctioned by Sotheby's during the Springells' lifetime, and others were disposed of separately. Today, when it is becoming more and more difficult to assemble a collection in this field, it seems almost miraculous to reflect on what was accomplished by the Springells, admittedly at a time when drawings of great quality were still coming onto the market at prices which seem like bargains to our generation.

Dr Springell was born in Prague at the end of the last century and studied to become an industrial chemist, but both music and the visual arts played a role in his life of almost equal importance to that of earning a living. For the young Springell, it was the work of the Bohemian engraver and topographical draughtsman Wenceslaus Hollar (1607–77) that provided the initial impetus to concentrate research and collecting-fever on drawings which had up to then not received the attention they deserved (Fig. 1). This interest led to the publication in 1938 of a book on Hollar's drawings which is still one of the most frequently consulted reference tools. Hollar eventually travelled to England, at the invitation of his great patron the Earl of Arundel, whom he had met in Cologne in the 1660s, accompanying him thence on an embassy to the Austrian emperor. When Springell, too, settled in this country, he took the opportunity to embark on further research on his hero and, with the help of the *Diary* by William Crowne and Arundel's letters, he traced this journey from Cologne to Vienna in a book, which was privately printed in 1963, entitled *Connoisseur and Diplomat*. It was splendidly illustrated with many Hollar drawings made on the trip, the kind also collected by Evelyn and Pepys, and now dispersed among various public collections, but of which eight belonged to Springell.

Building on their initial enthusiasm, the Springells decided to enlarge their collection and extend its range. They acquired drawings both from private sources and through the trade, and by the end of the war the collection comprised examples ranging from fourteenth-century miniatures to drawings by Manet and Whistler. Several items were lent to exhibitions at the Royal Academy, and in 1959 Colnaghi's organised a loan exhibition of over eighty of the Springell drawings, which opened the eyes of many visitors to the richness of the collection. There were drawings by Michelangelo, Dürer, Fra Bartolomeo, and an allegorical figure of *Justice* by Georg Pencz, based on an engraving by Marcantonio; a *naer het leven*

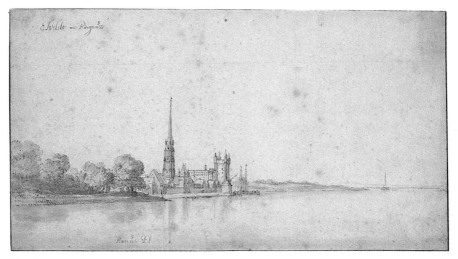

Fig. 1
Wenceslaus Hollar
VIEW OF ELTVILLE ON THE RHINE
Pen and brown ink and watercolour over traces of black chalk, inscribed in
brown ink, *circa* 1636, 6⅝in by 12⅛in (16.7cm by 30.7cm), £21,450 ($34,320)

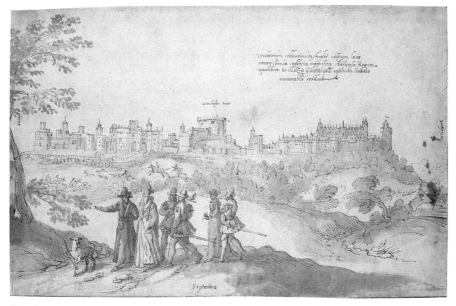

Fig. 2
Joris Hoefnagel
VIEW OF WINDSOR CASTLE WITH ELEGANT FIGURES IN THE FOREGROUND
Pen and brown ink and brown and blue wash, inscribed in brown ink,
circa 1568, 10⅜in by 16⅜in (26.4cm by 41.5cm), £63,800 ($102,080)

The drawings illustrated on this page are from the collection of the late Dr and
Mrs Francis Springell and were sold in London on 30 June 1986.

drawing of a peasant, then ascribed to Pieter Brueghel the Elder, is now known to be by Roelandt Savery. These vied with sheets by Aertsen, Rubens, Van Dyck, as well as a fine selection of eighteenth-century artists, among whom Giovanni Battista Tiepolo took pride of place.

In 1962 the Springells consigned to Sotheby's fifty-four of their major drawings. These included some splendid fourteenth- and fifteenth-century Italian and French miniatures, among them the impressive sheet with nine Old Testament Prophets and Kings (now in the Woodner Collection), with its interesting provenance from William Morris via Fairfax Murray to Sidney Cockerell, which Berenson thought was from the school of Fra Angelico, but is now believed to be possibly by the young Jean Fouquet. A large Michelangelo drawing identified by Johannes Wilde as *St Lawrence before the Prefect* of *circa* 1516, a study for a relief intended for the unexecuted façade of San Lorenzo, was already known from exhibitions at the Royal Academy, Colnaghi's and the British Museum. It had belonged to Mariette as well as to Sir Robert Witt, and it may be thought a kind of 'poetic justice' that it is now in the Courtauld Institute, together with so many of the Witt drawings, having been bequeathed to the Institute as part of the Princes' Gate Collection by the redoubtable collector, Count Antoine Seilern. Other distinguished drawings from that sale found their way into identifiable collections. The Stefano da Verona figure of *Charity* was acquired by the West Berlin Print Room, and the double-sided Fra Bartolomeo landscape, with the sketch of the Duomo of Siena on the reverse, from the Hesletine and Oppenheimer collections, is now in the National Gallery of Scotland in Edinburgh.

A further Fra Bartolomeo was the fine *Virgin and Child crowned by Angels*, a companion to another version in the Uffizi, whereas the Perugino *Baptism* was a study for the predella (now in Rouen) for the altar at S.Pietro in Perugia. A Carpaccio study of *Ecclesiastics* was related to the decorations of the Ducal Palace in Venice of 1507. The sheet with swirling *putti* was identified by Popham as a study by Giulio Campi for the Sforza altarpiece in S.Sigismondo at Cremona. Technically one of the most interesting drawings, and so desirable to collectors nowadays, was Castiglione's *Apollo and Marsyas* in brush and oil on paper.

Although the later seventeenth- and eighteenth-century drawings by Maratta, the two Tiepolo, Longhi and Guardi were retained, it is no longer clear why arguably the more distinguished section of the Italians were then being sold. It is possible that the greater reliance on the advice of the late Edmund Schilling, whose expertise lay more in the direction of the northern schools, was one reason. He steered the Springells towards the Dürer drawings (Fig. 3) and towards the enchanting *View of Windsor* (Fig. 2) by the sixteenth-century Flemish artist Joris Hoefnagel. This is the sketch for a more fully worked-out drawing in the Royal Collection, from which Braun and Hogenberg made their engraving, which they included in the *Civitates Orbis Terrarum*, published in Cologne in 1572. The Springell drawing must have formed part of a sketchbook of 'towns and castles from nature in addition to costumes', which van Mander mentions in his *Schilderboek* (Haarlem 1604). Other drawings from the sketchbook are in the National Library at Vienna.

Fig. 3
Albrecht Dürer
CHRIST BEING NAILED TO THE CROSS
Pen and brown ink, signed with monogram, *circa* 1504, 11⅝in by 8⅛in (29.4cm by 20.5cm)
London £165,000 ($264,000). 30.VI.86
From the collection of the late Dr and Mrs Francis Springell

Fig. 4
Antoine Watteau
STUDIES OF A GIRL'S HEAD AND OF A KITTEN
Red chalk and black chalk, *circa* 1717, 7¾in by 4⅞in (19.6cm by 12.3cm)
London £126,500 ($202,400). 30.VI.86

The drawings illustrated on these pages are from the collection of the late Dr and
Mrs Francis Springell.

Fig. 5
James Abbott McNeill Whistler
STREET SCENE IN CHELSEA
Watercolour, *circa* 1888, 5in by 8½in (12.6cm by 21.7cm)
London £79,200 ($126,720). 30.VI.86

The scope of the collection was widened to include some distinguished examples of the French School from Claude to Saint-Aubin, Boucher, Fragonard and Watteau (Fig. 4) were added to the collection. There was a drawing by the young Renoir, dating from when he was still decorating porcelains and fans, as well as a brush drawing by Manet for the Munich *Le déjeuner*, a sheet that at one time had belonged to the Springell's neighbour at Keswick, Sir Hugh Walpole. But British artists were also collected, and there were interesting sheets by Reynolds, Gainsborough, Rowlandson and a watercolour by Whistler (Fig. 5).

The Springells did not amass drawings haphazardly. Each acquisition was properly researched and a file with all the information they had gathered was always made readily available to those who showed an interest. Correspondence and advice came from such varied sources as Professors Panofsky, Pächt and Charles Mitchell, from A.E. Popham, Ludwig Burchard and of course from Edmund Schilling. In many ways it is sad to think that a collection assembled with such care and devotion should now have been dispersed to the four winds. But no doubt many of the sheets will now have found homes with other enthusiasts, who have rejoiced both in the chase and capture of their new possessions.

Hans Leonhard Schäufelein
SELF PORTRAIT
Black chalk with later grey wash, signed with monogram, *circa* 1510, 7in by 5in
(17.7cm by 12.7cm), £132,000 ($211,200)

The drawings illustrated on these pages are from the collection of the late Dr and
Mrs Francis Springell and were sold in London on 30 June 1986.

Rembrandt Harmensz. van Rijn
AN ARTIST IN HIS STUDIO
Pen and brown ink, *circa* 1633, 8⅛in by 6⅝in (20.5cm by 17cm), £341,000 ($545,600)

Jacopo Ligozzi
PERSIAN WITH A CAMEL
Tempera heightened with gold, *circa* 1580, 10⅝in by 8½in (27cm by 21.5cm)
New York $50,600 (£35,385). 16.I.86

Hendrick Goltzius
VENUS, ADONIS AND CUPID
Pen, brown ink and wash heightened with white on brown prepared paper,
signed with monogram and dated *1600*, 7¾in by 5in (19.6cm by 12.7cm)
Amsterdam DFl1,035,000 (£236,842:$352,895). 18.XI.85

Francesco Guardi
VIEW OF THE GRAND CANAL WITH SAN SIMEONE PICCOLO AND SANTA LUCIA
Pen and brown ink and wash over black chalk, $11\frac{1}{2}$in by $21\frac{1}{8}$in (29.2cm by 53.6cm)
London £40,700 ($65,120). 30.VI.86

Jean-Baptiste Greuze
STUDY FOR THE NOTARY IN 'L'ACCORDÉE DU VILLAGE'
Black chalk and charcoal over red chalk heightened with white, signed, *circa* 1761,
16¾in by 17⅛in (42.6cm by 43.5cm)
Monte Carlo FF943,500 (£91,602:$133,640). 22.II.86

Opposite
Giovanni Battista Lusieri
VIEW OF MERGELLINA
Pen, black ink and watercolour over pencil, 21½in by 34¼in (54.5cm by 86.9cm)
London £74,800 ($119,680). 30.VI.86
From the collection of The Earl of Elgin and Kincardine, KT

Joseph Wright of Derby, ARA
A GROTTO IN THE KINGDOM OF NAPLES, WITH BANDITTI: A SUNSET
Circa 1777, 48in by 68½in (122cm by 174cm)
London £1,210,000 ($1,948,100). 9.VII.86

Wright and his wife left England for Italy in November 1773 and after brief stops in Nice and
Genoa landed finally at Leghorn in 1774, from where they travelled overland to Rome. After
working for several months in the city, Wright began to explore the ancient sites of Pompeii,
Herculaneum and Mount Vesuvius. He also sketched Virgil's tomb on the hill above Naples and
visited the grottoes in the Gulf of Salerno. This picture was inspired by the stupendous sights of
these grottoes, which haunted Joseph Wright's imagination long after his return to England.
Grotto with Banditti was not only the most spectacular of his paintings on this theme, but also one
of his most poetic landscapes.

Derby Aug.t 29.th 00

Sir,

Within I have sent
you a Bill of the two
Pictures, the discharging
of w.ch I beg you will consider your own conveniency

I am
Sir
Your much obliged
Hhble Serv.t
Jos.h Wright

Two Caverns in the Gulf
of Salernum. The one w.th
a Banditti, one hundred &
fifty Guineas. The other
with the Figure of Julia
one hundred Guineas ——

Joseph Wright's bill for *A Grotto in the Kingdom of Naples, with Banditti: a Sunset*, which he sold to Josiah Cockshutt, in 1780, for the enormous sum of one hundred and fifty guineas.

Arthur Devis

PORTRAIT OF WILLS, FIRST MARQUESS OF DOWNSHIRE WITH HIS WIFE MARGARETTA AND THEIR TWO
CHILDREN, LORD ARTHUR AND LADY MARY AMELIA
24in by 29½in (61cm by 75cm)
London £143,000 ($221,650). 12.III.86
From the collection of the Marchioness of Downshire Settlement

Opposite
Sir Joshua Reynolds, PRA
SIMPLICITY – PORTRAIT OF MISS THEOPHILA GWATKIN
29½in by 25in (75cm by 63.5cm)
London £242,000 ($375,100). 12.III.86

John Frederick Herring, Senior
THE STREATLAM STUD
Signed and dated *1836*, and inscribed *Brood Mares and Foals the property of J. Bowes, Esq.* on a label
on the stretcher, 42in by 62in (106.7cm by 157.5cm)
New York $836,000 (£561,074). 5.VI.86
From the collection of the late Charles J. Cronan, Jr

Jan Wyck
A HUNTSMAN COURSING WITH A PACK OF HOUNDS ABOVE BERKHAMSTED, HERTFORDSHIRE
Signed, 39in by 45in (99cm by 114.5cm)
London £319,000 ($494,450). 12.III.86

John Cleveley
AN EXTENSIVE VIEW OF THE DOCKYARDS AT DEPTFORD
Signed and dated *1774*, 35½in by 59in (90cm by 150cm)
London £116,600 ($180,730). 12.III.86
From the collection of the Rt. Hon the Earl of Wharncliffe

Opposite
English School
A PROSPECT OF LITTLECOTE HOUSE IN THE COUNTY OF WILTSHIRE FROM THE SOUTH
On panel, *circa* 1710, 45in by 91in (114.3cm by 231cm)
London £154,000 ($232,540). 21.XI.85

Attributed to William van der Hagen
A PROSPECT OF WEALD HALL IN THE COUNTY OF ESSEX
113in by 191in (287.5cm by 485cm)
London £143,000 ($213,070). 20.XI.85

Joseph Mallord William Turner, RA

THE CHANNEL SKETCHBOOK

One of seventy-four watercolours and twenty-six pencil studies of the setting sun, clouds and the coast, on wove paper, *circa* 1845, each leaf 3¾in by 6¼in (9.5cm by 16cm)
London £528,000 ($850,080). 10.VII.86

These sketches were probably made during the summer and autumn of 1845, when Turner visited the Channel coasts of Kent and Normandy. In them he sought to capture shifting configurations of sea and sky, one of his life-long obsessions. Page 82 verso, illustrated above, is one of many sketches which incorporate other elements such as shipping, shown here at sunset. Figures, breakwaters, whalers, a harbour and a domed tower appear in other sketches. The sketchbook originally belonged to Mr Pound, son of Mrs Booth, Turner's housekeeper for many years. Like other items with a Booth family provenance, it probably escaped inclusion in Turner's bequest of drawings and paintings to the nation because of its 'unfinished' quality. Time has reversed the judgement on such work; the rapid notations of the *Channel Sketchbook* are now highly valued for the technical and colouristic brilliance with which Turner strove to set down the fleeting effects of nature.

Opposite
Thomas Gainsborough, RA

STUDY OF A LADY SEATED, WEARING A STRAW BONNET

Black chalk heightened with white chalk on blue laid paper; with a black chalk study of a girl seated on a bank on the reverse, *circa* 1770, 12½in by 9⅜in (31.7cm by 23.8cm)
London £220,000 ($352,000). 30.VI.86
From the collection of the late Dr and Mrs Francis Springell

Thomas Girtin
A VILLAGE ON THE RIVER EXE
Watercolour over pencil, signed, *circa* 1799, $11\frac{3}{4}$in by $20\frac{1}{2}$in (30cm by 52cm)
London £55,000 ($83,050). 21.XI.85
From the collection of the late Miss K.G. Robinson

Thomas Shotter Boys
PARIS FROM THE RIVER SEINE
Watercolour over pencil, heightened with bodycolour and scratching out, $9\frac{1}{4}$in by $22\frac{7}{8}$in
(23.5cm by 58cm)
London £55,000 ($84,700). 13.III.86

John Constable, RA
STANWAY MILL, NEAR COLCHESTER, ESSEX
8¼in by 6⅛in (21cm by 15.5cm)
London £61,600 ($99,176). 10.VII.86
From the collection of Dr Donald M. Irvine

William Kent
A chinoiserie garden temple, one of
thirty-nine designs for Esher Place,
Surrey, and its park and garden buildings.
Sold by private treaty to the Victoria
and Albert Museum for £170,000
($266,900). 28.V.86

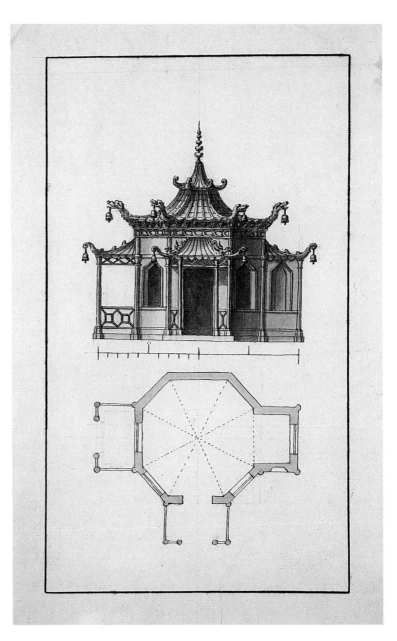

Opposite, above
Chinese School
VIEW OF THE HONGS AT CANTON
Gouache on silk laid on canvas, *circa* 1760, 18¼in by 30⅞in (46.5cm by 78.5cm)
London £13,200 ($19,800). 6.XI.85

Opposite, below
Studio of Ting Qua
VOLUME OF WATERCOLOURS
One of forty-four views, watercolour heightened with bodycolour and gum arabic, 9in by 14¼in (23cm by 36cm)
London £36,300 ($54,450). 6.XI.85

William Holman Hunt, OM, RWS
THE FLIGHT OF MADELINE AND PORPHYRO DURING THE DRUNKENNESS ATTENDING THE REVELRY
Compositional study, pencil, inscribed on the reverse by Edith Holman Hunt, *circa* 1848,
5⅜in by 7¾in (13.5cm by 19.5cm)
London £17,600 ($25,872). 10.X.85

Opposite
Sketch for the left-hand side of the same composition, oil and pencil on board, inscribed on the
reverse, *circa* 1848, 10½in by 7½in (26.5cm by 19cm)
London £38,500 ($56,595). 10.X.85

The study and sketch illustrated on these pages are from the collection of Mrs Elisabeth Burt.

Frederic Lord Leighton, PRA, RWS, HRCA, HRSW
EUCHARIS
Signed with initials, and titled on labels attached to the stretcher,
circa 1863, 33in by 22¾in (84cm by 58cm)
London £154,000 ($243,320). 17.VI.86

James Jacques Tissot
THE RUBENS HAT
Signed, 36in by 25in (91.5cm by 63.5cm)
London £308,000 ($486,640). 17.VI.86

Albert Joseph Moore, ARWS
AN IDYLL
Study in black chalks, 32½in by 28¾in (82.5cm by 73cm)
London £11,000 ($16,170). 10.X.85

Opposite
Albert Joseph Moore, ARWS
MUSK
Signed twice with anthemion, 27in by 19¾in (68.5cm by 50cm)
London £154,000 ($243,320). 17.VI.86

Sir Alfred Munnings, PRA
THE HUNTSMAN
Signed, 20in by 24¼in (50.8cm by 61.5cm)
New York $110,000 (£73,826). 5.VI.86
From the collection of George Strawbridge, Jr

Sir Alfred Munnings, PRA
SHRIMP, A GROOM, LEADING HORSES
21¾in by 26¼in (55.3cm by 66.7cm)
New York $143,000 (£95,973). 5.VI.86

Spencer Gore
THE ALHAMBRA
20⅛in by 24in (51cm by 61cm)
London £48,400 ($76,956). 21.V.86

The Alhambra in Leicester Square was the most popular of the music halls. This picture, probably painted in 1909, shows a scene from the ballet *Paquita*, a Spanish gypsy story, which was produced in 1908.

Opposite
Frank Dobson, RA
THE RATION PARTY
Signed and dated '*19*, 29½in by 24⅝in (75cm by 62.5cm)
London £50,600 ($74,888). 13.XI.85

Sir Alfred Munnings, PRA
GYPSIES
Signed, *circa* 1915, 26in by 30¾in (66cm by 78cm)
London £60,500 ($96,195). 21.V.86

Opposite
Sir George Clausen, RA
LITTLE KITTY
Signed, titled and dated *1925* on the reverse, 25in by 20⅞in (63.5cm by 53cm)
London £48,400 ($76,956). 21.V.86
From the collection of the late Dennis Hadwick

Louis-Léopold Boilly
A BOULEVARD SCENE
On panel, signed and dated *1806*, 9½in by 13in (24cm by 33cm)
Monte Carlo FF2,109,000 (£204,757:$298,725). 22.II.86

Opposite
Jean-Auguste-Dominique Ingres
PORTRAIT OF THE HONORABLE SIR FLEETWOOD BROUGHTON REYNOLDS PELLEW
Pencil on paper, signed, inscribed and dated *Del à Rome 1817*, 12in by 8¾in (30.5cm by 22.3cm)
New York $286,000 (£186,928). 14.V.86
From the collection of the late Etta E. Steinberg and the late Florence S. Weil

Opposite
Théodore Géricault
PORTRAIT OF A YOUNG MAN
Circa 1816, 17⅞in by 14⅜in (45.5cm by 36.5cm)
London £275,000 ($434,500). 17.VI.86

Théodore Géricault
VENUS AND CUPID *recto*
A CLASSICAL WARRIOR *verso*
Pen, brown ink and watercolour heightened
with white bodycolour, *circa* 1815, 7⅝in by 10¼in
(19.5cm by 26cm)
London £35,200 ($53,856). 26.XI.85

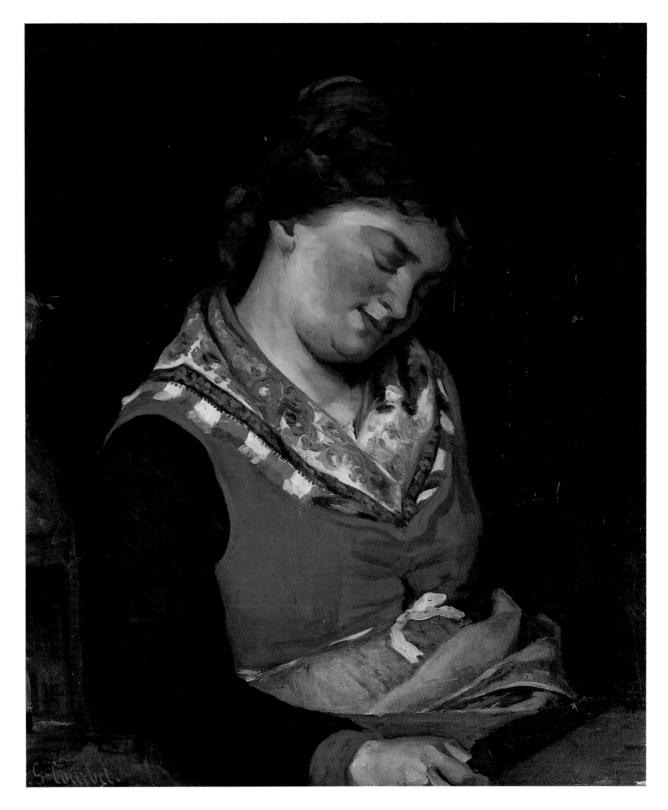

Jean-François Millet
BERGÈRE ET SON TROUPEAU, AU FOND LA TOUR DU MOULIN DE CHAILLY
Signed, 1873, 37in by 46¾in (94cm by 118.8cm)
New York $506,000 (£339,597). 22.V.86

Opposite
Gustave Courbet
SLEEPING PEASANT WOMAN
Signed, 1853, 26⅝in by 22½in (67.5cm by 57cm)
London £126,500 ($193,545). 26.XI.85

Max Liebermann
ON THE MONTE PINCIO, ROME
Signed and dated '*11*, 27⅛in by 39in (69cm by 99cm)
London £99,000 ($156,420). 17.VI.86

Opposite
Emil Jakob Schindler
THE BRIDGE AT GOISERN
Signed twice and dated *1881* and *1885*, 38¼in by 33⅛in (97cm by 84.5cm)
London £82,500 ($126,225). 26.XI.85

Jean Béraud
LE THÉÂTRE FRANÇAIS, PARIS
Signed and dated *1878*, 25½in by 32in (64.7cm by 81.2cm)
New York $220,000 (£153,846). 31.X.85
From the collection of the late Princess Elizabeth Jenny Rospigliosi

Opposite
Giovanni Boldini
PORTRAIT OF SIGNORINA CONCHA DE OSSA
Pastel on prepared canvas, signed and dated *1888*, 87in by 47½in (221.6cm by 120.7cm)
New York $148,500 (£99,664). 22.V.86

Christen Købke
FIGURES ON THE NORDRE KASTELSBRO AT SUNSET
1837, 17⅛in by 25in (43.5cm by 63.5cm)
London £286,000 ($451,880). 17.VI.86

Vilhelm Hammershoi
INTERIOR OF THE ARTIST'S HOME AT 25 BREDGADE, COPENHAGEN
Signed with monogram and titled on the stretcher, *circa* 1911, 28in by 25¼in
(71.1cm by 64.2cm)
New York $90,750 (£60,906). 22.V.86

Works by Matisse in the Bakwin Collection

John L. Tancock

It is not often that major works by Henri Matisse appear at auction. Although he was prolific in many media, most of his masterpieces are already the pride of public and private collections throughout the world. The sale of selected works from the estate of Dr Ruth Morris Bakwin, which included three sculptures executed between 1908 and 1911, two of which are discussed here, and two paintings, was consequently a remarkable occasion. Only a portion of the collection formed by Dr Harry and Dr Ruth Morris Bakwin was sold at auction, important works by Van Gogh and Cézanne among others, had been bequeathed before the sale took place, but the group of works by Matisse accurately represents the high standards that had been set in the formation of the collection.

Matisse's sculptural oeuvre extended over a period of fifty-six years and consists of only sixty-nine works which, with the exception of the four reliefs known collectively as *The backs*, are mostly modest in scale. What has fascinated art historians in recent years is not the innovatory use of materials or subject matter, both of which are quite conventional, but rather the extraordinary diversity of formal approaches adopted by Matisse as his sculpture developed in tandem with his painting. 'I practised sculpture, or rather modelling,' Matisse said, 'as a complementary study to put my ideas in order.' And, indeed, the sporadic appearance of his three-dimensional work coincides with the periods in his painting when most problems had to be solved. Matisse met Rodin around 1898 and, while not rejecting his modelling technique, strongly criticised Rodin's lack of architectural feeling, stating that in contrast in his own works he 'could only envisage the general architecture . . . replacing explanatory details by a living and suggestive synthesis.' On the other hand, the static, volumetric approach of Maillol, who categorically rejected the melodramatic character of Rodin's art, was no more to his liking. Contrasting Maillol's swelling volumes with his own 'arabesque', Matisse stated that 'Maillol did not like risks and I was drawn to them. He did not like adventure.'

Thus by 1908, when Matisse executed *Two negresses* and *Decorative figure* (Fig. 1), he was already the exponent of an approach to modelling that was highly idiosyncratic, having rejected as much as he had absorbed from the leading sculptors of his time. The school he opened in the former Couvent du Sacré Coeur, close to the Hôtel Biron where Rodin was living, attracted pupils from all over the world. His eloquent *Notes d'un peintre* were published in *La Grande Revue*, vol. 52, December 25

Fig. 1
Henri Matisse
DECORATIVE FIGURE
Bronze, stamped with initials and the foundry mark *C. Valsuani cire perdue*, numbered *2/10*,
dated *août 1908*, height 28⅛in (71.5cm)
New York $1,045,000 (£735,915). 13.XI.85
From the collection of the late Dr Ruth Morris Bakwin

1908, the same year that Sarah Stein took notes in his classes. He instructed his students to approach the models with no preconceived ideas and to 'express by masses in relation to one another and large sweeps of line in interrelation.' The expression of movement was to be avoided unless the sculptor had full comprehension of the entire movement of which he could represent only a part.

During 1908 Matisse worked on the frieze-like *Bathers with a turtle* (City Art Museum, St Louis). The Bakwin sculptures of the same year share the monumental calm of the three figures contemplating the turtle; the sweeping elisions of the models' anatomies and the sure command of three-dimensional form reveal Matisse's confidence in handling two-dimensional and three-dimensional expression. Indeed, *Two negresses* could almost be taken as a textbook demonstration, since its source was a photograph taken from a French ethnographical periodical showing 'Deux jeunes filles Targui.'

In addition to clarifying his ideas, Matisse's sculpture was also a useful adjunct to many of the paintings executed before 1916–17. Transformed and occasionally dematerialised, the sculptures frequently introduced a human element into compositions that otherwise lacked such associations. *Two negresses* appeared two years later in *Fruit and bronze* (Pushkin Museum of Fine Arts, Moscow) and the statuesque *Decorative figure* appeared in a number of key pictures, including *The red studio*, 1911 (Museum of Modern Art, New York), *The pink studio*, 1911 (Pushkin Museum of Fine Arts, Moscow) and *Piano lesson*, 1916 (Museum of Modern Art, New York).

Of the two paintings from the Bakwin collection, one was painted in 1919 and summarises the themes that were to occupy Matisse during his Nice period, and the other was a superb portrait from the 1930s. Matisse spoke on many occasions of the crucial role played by the model in the creation of a work of art. *The artist and his model* (Fig. 2), depicted such an encounter. Matisse's first trip to Nice occurred in December 1916 but it was not until 1918 that he found the rooms in the Hôtel de la Méditerranée that were to provide a haven from the rigours of the Parisian winter for the next three years. Although Matisse painted views of his immediate environment and the countryside around Nice, his most characteristic paintings for the next decade were of the rooms in which he was staying, although the existence of a world outside this hermetic environment was frequently alluded to by a view through a window. A 1918 *Self portrait* (Private collection), one of the last pictures in the severe manner that had characterised Matisse's art since 1910, depicted the artist in his formal suit, easel in hand, glaring rather balefully at the spectator. In a sombre-hued, austere work of 1916, *The painter and his model* (Musée National d'Art Moderne, Centre Georges Pompidou, Paris), the encounter between Matisse and the model Laurette took place in the studio on the Quai St Michel, but the resulting picture had less to do with the artist's observation of his model than with the construction of a memorable pictorial scaffolding.

Matisse's mood had changed by 1918. Whereas at the beginning of the war he spent time in the company of Picasso and Juan Gris, he now paid occasional visits to Bonnard at Antibes and took some of his paintings to show to the aged Renoir

Fig. 2
Henri Matisse
THE ARTIST AND HIS MODEL IN THE STUDIO
Signed, 1919, $23\frac{5}{8}$in by $28\frac{3}{4}$in (60cm by 73cm)
New York $1,155,000 (£813,380). 13.XI.85
From the collection of the late Dr Ruth Morris Bakwin

at Cagnes. These meetings indicate the different ambiance in which Matisse now chose to work. His austere style gave way to a phase when his chosen environment and subject-matter, the one inseparable from the other, resulted in a more harmonious mode of expression. In the Bakwin painting there is an apparent lack of formal inventiveness. The diffused southern light caresses and softens the forms and the artist's searching eye, scrutinising the form of his model, is now turned away from the spectator. Writing in 1951, Alfred Barr commented that paintings such as this seemed 'minor and casual' if compared with the 1916 *Painter and model*, but thirty-

five years later the poise of such works is widely admired and seen not as a slackening of the creative impulse but as a rich episode in its own right.

By the end of the 1920s Matisse was restless. In the spring of 1930 he travelled to Tahiti and shortly after accepted commissions that took him away from his easel and canvas. Albert Skira commissioned illustrations for an edition of the poems of Mallarmé and the challenge of working on the greatly reduced scale of the page and in black and white provided a stimulus that resulted in some of Matisse's most intensely felt images. In June 1931 he accepted a commission for three lunettes over French windows in the Barnes Foundation, Merion. Returning to the theme of the dance, which had resulted in the great painting of 1909–10 (Hermitage Museum, Leningrad), Matisse worked on a scale that was new to him, drawing directly on the canvas with a charcoal pencil attached to the end of a long bamboo pole, in a more impersonal style suitable for the architectural setting. Thus by 1934, when the allure of oil on canvas returned, Matisse had evolved a greatly simplified style that could be used in distilled form on the pages of a book and on a monumental scale, as in the Barnes Foundation murals.

But grand simplicity does not come easily. Deceptively simple works such as *The dream* (Musée Nationale d'Art Moderne, Centre Georges Pompidou, Paris) and *Pink nude* (Baltimore Museum of Art, Cone Collection), both of 1935, for which the model was Lydia Delectorskaya, evolved tortuously. Matisse liked to record the various stages in the development of his works and this was the case with *The blue blouse* (Fig. 3), 1936, which again departed from the features of the faithful Russian model and amanuensis. Four states were illustrated in *Minotaure* in 1936 showing the progression from a relatively naturalistic and tentative beginning to the grand simplicity of the final version. Matisse described how at each stage of the development of his image there was a certain equilibrium, but when resuming work, if a weakness were detected, he would 're-enter through the breach' and reconsider the entire work, hence the extraordinary transformations. In the same conversation he spoke of pictures that have become 'refinements, subtle gradations, dissolutions without energy . . . which call for beautiful blues, reds, yellows – matter to stir the sensual depths in man. This is the starting point of Fauvism: to return to the purity of means.' *The blue blouse* is a fine example of the classic balance Matisse had evolved in the 1930s, a balance between refinement and sensuality, simplicity of form and richness of association.

Matisse's devotion to the female form as the principal inspiration of his art did not change significantly throughout the more than six decades of his career. The Bakwin bronzes and paintings showed how diverse in character were the works that resulted from this lifelong obsession.

Fig. 3, *opposite*
Henri Matisse
THE BLUE BLOUSE
Signed and dated *36*, 36¼in by 23⅝in (92cm by 60cm)
New York $1,430,000 (£1,007,043). 13.XI.85
From the collection of the late Dr Ruth Morris Bakwin

Edgar Degas
CHEVAL AU GALOP SUR LE PIED DROIT
Bronze, signed, numbered *47/D* and stamped with the foundry mark *A.A. Hébrard, cire perdue*,
height 12⅛in (31cm)
London £253,000 ($399,740). 24.VI.86

Opposite
Edgar Degas
LA FAMILLE MANTE
Pastel on paper, signed, *circa* 1889, 35¾in by 19⅝in (89.9cm by 49.9cm)
New York $1,650,000 (£1,071,429). 13.V.86